Readings in Literary Criticism 12

CRITICS ON MELVILLE

Readings in Literary Criticism

CRITICS ON MELVILLE

Readings in Literary Criticism
Edited by Thomas J. Rountree

University of Miami Press
Coral Gables, Florida

CONTENTS

ACKNOWLEDGMENTS

Newton Arvin: from *Herman Melville*. Copyright 1950 by William Sloane Associates, Inc. Reprinted by permission of William Morrow and Company, Inc.

W. H. Auden: from *The Collected Shorter Poems, 1927-1957*. Copyright © 1940, renewed 1968 by W. H. Auden. Reprinted by permission of Random House, Inc.

Thornton Y. Booth: from *Nineteenth-Century Fiction*, vol. 17, no. 1, 1962. Copyright © 1962 by The Regents of the University of California. Reprinted by permission of the author and The Regents.

Robert M. Farnsworth: from the *Bulletin of The New York Public Library*, vol. 65, 1961. Copyright © 1961 by The New York Public Library. Reprinted by permission of the author and the publisher.

Charles Feidelson, Jr.: from *Symbolism and American Literature*. Copyright © 1953 by The University of Chicago Press. Reprinted by permission of the author and the publisher.

Joseph J. Firebaugh: from *Nineteenth-Century Fiction*, vol. 9, no. 2, 1954. Copyright © 1954 by The Regents of the University of California. Reprinted by permission of the author and The Regents.

Richard Harter Fogle: from *Tulane Studies in English*, vol. 11, 1961. Copyright © 1961 by *Tulane Studies in English*. Reprinted by permission of the publisher.

H. Bruce Franklin: from *The Wake of the Gods: Melville's Mythology*. Copyright © 1963 by the Board of Trustees of the Leland Stanford Junior University. Reprinted by permission of the Stanford University Press.

Charles G. Hoffmann: from *The South Atlantic Quarterly*, vol. 52, 1953. Copyright © 1953 by Duke University Press. Reprinted by permission of the publisher.

D. H. Lawrence: from *Studies in Classic American Literature*. Copyright 1923, renewed 1951 by Frieda Lawrence. Reprinted by permission of The Viking Press, Inc.

Harry Levin: from *The Power of Blackness*. Copyright © 1958 by Harry Levin. Reprinted by permission of Alfred A. Knopf, Inc.

R. W. B. Lewis: from *The American Adam*. Copyright © 1955 by The University of Chicago Press. Reprinted by permission of the author and the publisher.

F. O. Matthiessen: from *American Renaissance*. Copyright © 1941 by Oxford University Press, Inc. Reprinted by permission of the publisher.

Paul McCarthy: from *The Emerson Society Quarterly*, no. 33, 1963. Copyright © 1963 by The Emerson Society. Reprinted by permission of the publisher.

James E. Miller, Jr.: from *The Journal of English and Germanic Philology*, vol. 58, 1959. Copyright © 1959 by the University of Illinois Press. Reprinted by permission of the publisher.

Milton Millhauser: from *The Journal of Aesthetics and Art Criticism*, vol. 13, 1955. Copyright © 1955 by The American Society for Aesthetics. Reprinted by permission of the author and the publisher.

V. L. Parrington: from *Main Currents in American Thought*, Vol. II. Copyright © 1927 by Harcourt Brace Jovanovich, Inc. Reprinted by permission of the publisher.

Robert E. Spiller: from *The Cycle of American Literature*. Copyright © 1955 by Macmillan. Reprinted by permission of the publisher.

Milton R. Stern: from *The Fine Hammered Steel of Herman Melville*. Copyright © 1957 by the University of Illinois Press. Reprinted by permission of the publisher.

Randall Stewart: from "Hawthorne's Contributions to *The Salem Advertiser*," *American Literature*, vol. 5, 1934. Copyright © 1934 by Duke University Press. Reprinted by permission of the publisher.

Lawrance Thompson: from *Melville's Quarrel with God*. Copyright 1952 by Princeton University Press; 1967, Princeton Paperback. Reprinted by permission of the publisher.

Howard P. Vincent: from *The New England Quarterly*, vol. 22, 1949. Copyright © 1949 by *The New England Quarterly*. Reprinted by permission of the author and the publisher.

E. L. Grant Watson: from *The New England Quarterly*, vol. 3, 1930. Copyright © 1930 by *The New England Quarterly*. Reprinted by permission of the publisher.

Charles Weir, Jr.: from "Malice Reconciled; A Note on Melville's *Billy Budd*," *University of Toronto Quarterly*, vol. 13, 1944. Copyright © 1944 by the *University of Toronto Quarterly*. Reprinted by permission of the University of Toronto Press.

INTRODUCTION

SINCE "the quest" is a major theme in the works of Melville, it is perhaps fitting that a student of the criticism concerning these works faces a quest also—not from a scarcity of critiques but from an abundance. Such, however, was not always the case. For while critical response, beginning with the publication of *Typee* in 1846, led to a varying rise of mixed voices in the 1840s and 1850s, it was followed by a decline which for six decades amounted to almost unbroken silence until, in the 1920s, the Melville revival began a new and still growing critical response.

During the midnineteenth-century decade of Melville's most sustained literary effort, his books received more critical notice than the newly alerted twentieth-century critics at first thought. The first two, *Typee* and *Omoo* (1847), were immediate successes and, though some reviewers were scandalized by Melville's "voluptuousness" and his uncomplimentary comments on the missionaries in Polynesia, the books were generally praised. The allegorical inventions in *Mardi* (1849), while receiving limited applause from Bayard Taylor, brought from others cries of confusion and exasperation. *Redburn* (1849) and *White-Jacket* (1850) won back some of Melville's audience, and at first so did *Moby-Dick* (1851). While many of the first British and American reviewers criticized the latter for its nonconformity to accepted canons of the novel and for its impiety, some lauded its philosophy and almost all found praise for its graphic sea and whaling scenes. These early tendencies toward extreme praise or censure narrowed within a year to a definitely adverse reaction—related perhaps to the assaults on *Pierre* (1852)—until after 1857 *Moby-Dick* received silent neglect for many years, as did Melville's works generally after the initial responses to *Israel Potter* (1855), the *Piazza Tales* (1856), and *The Confidence-Man* (1857). A notable exception came from British writer W. Clark Russell, but not until 1892, and it proved to be only an obituary ripple in the long silence.

The neglect has now been compensated. Beginning with the first comprehensive survey of Melville's writings (F. J. Mather, Jr.'s "Herman Melville" in the *Weekly Review* of 1919) and with the first full-length biography (Raymond M. Weaver's *Herman Melville: Mariner and Mystic* of 1921), the 1920s initiated a critical rediscovery that has been growing steadily for half a century. The depth and allusiveness of Melville's writing have challenged the research and acumen of eminent minds on both sides of the Atlantic. Numerous books of scholarship and biography have resulted, and the critical articles have multiplied. According to one survey, some 500 articles on Melville had appeared in the forty years to 1960. Another tabulation showed that by 1962 almost 300 critical essays (ranging from a few pages to book-length treatment) on *Moby-Dick* alone had been published in America and Britain, exclusive of incidental reviews, foreign studies (Oriental as well as European), handbook discussions, and introductions to reprint editions. Now, only nine years later, the number of essays on *Moby-Dick* has almost doubled, while other Melville studies also increase yearly—as attested by the periodic bibliographies of journals like *American Literature* and *Publications of the Modern Language Association.*

The student of Melville criticism thus faces a quest, and it is the design of this book to aid in the search by offering material now difficult of access and by presenting a reasonable cross section of critical approaches.

The first part of the book tenders early reviews that often can be found only in the dimmer recesses of the larger libraries. I have aimed to illustrate that the early reactions were mixed, often so within a single critique, for it still seems worthwhile to combat the notion that Melville received little or no response in his major creative decade. On the other hand, I have included George Washington Peck's attack on *Pierre* because it represents Peck's usual vitriolic attitude toward Melville's works and because it is symptomatic of the general reception of *Pierre* in 1852. I have identified the early critics whenever possible, but a parenthetic question mark follows a reviewer's name if there is any doubt.

Parts two and three focus on the continuing Melville revival. In "Perspectives" are selections which should enable the reader to move to the full-length treatments with a perspective that invites both allowances and reservations. Like these selections, the essays in part three give a variety of critical emphases: on the whole work or a significant part, on the biographical, the psychological, the religious, the symbolic, the mythic, the archetypal, the thematic, the formal, the tonal. I have made no effort to regularize certain matters: for instance, Melville's great novel is entitled *Moby Dick* or *Moby-Dick* according to the critic writing. Likewise I have not interfered with the earlier misprint of *soiled* for *coiled* in the phrase "soiled fish of the sea" in *White-Jacket,* but have left it as the critic knew and used the quotation. My goal has been the accuracy of variety, perhaps not inappropriate to the ambiguities of Melville.

The purpose of this collection is to help a reader enjoy and understand the fiction and poetry of Melville. To my mind there is no one study of the man and his work with which a student should begin and to which he should finally return above all others. The real starting point is Melville's writing. This book can assist intermediately and can point the way to other assistance. Ultimately, of course, the reader must return to Melville's novels, short stories, and poems, for therein lies the greater quest.

University of South Alabama, 1971   THOMAS J. ROUNTREE

TABLE OF IMPORTANT DATES

1850   Published *White-Jacket.*

1850-1863   Lived at "Arrowhead," his newly purchased farm near Pitts-
                field, Massachusetts. Became friend of Nathaniel Hawthorne,
                a neighbor during his first two years there.

1851   Published *Moby-Dick,* dedicated to Hawthorne.

1852   Published *Pierre.* Probably suffered near breakdown after fin-
                ishing book.

1855   Published *Israel Potter.*

1856   Published *The Piazza Tales* ("Benito Cereno," "The Encanta-
                das," "Bartleby the Scrivener," and others). Journeyed to the
                Holy Land via Liverpool (to visit Hawthorne, then consul) and
                Constantinople.

1857   Returned to the United States. Published *The Confidence-Man.*
                Began lecturing intermittently in the East and Middle West.

1860   Embarked from New York for San Francisco and Manila on
                the merchant ship captained by his brother Thomas, but re-
                turned home from San Francisco.

1861   Failed to obtain a U. S. Consular Service appointment.

1863   Sold "Arrowhead" and moved to New York City.

1866   Published *Battle-Pieces,* his first collection of poems.

1866-1885   Worked as a district inspector of customs.

1867   His first son Malcolm committed suicide.

1876   Published *Clarel.*

1885   Made financially comfortable through family bequests.

1886   His second son Stanwix, alone in a San Francisco hospital, died
                after a long illness.

1888   Published *John Marr and Other Sailors.*

1889   Engaged during winter or spring in the final version of *Billy
                Budd,* which he was still revising at his death and which was
                not published until 1924.

1891   Published *Timoleon.* Died September 28 in New York City.

Early Reviews

NATHANIEL HAWTHORNE: 1846

WILEY & PUTNAM'S LIBRARY OF AMERICAN BOOKS, NOS. XIII AND XIV. The present numbers of this excellent and popular series, contain a very remarkable work, entitled *'Typee, or a Peep at Polynesian Life.'* It records the adventures of a young American who ran away from a whale ship at the Marquesas, and spent some months as the guest, or captive, of a native tribe, of which scarcely anything had been hitherto known to the civilized world.— The book is lightly but vigorously written; and we are acquainted with no work that gives a freer and more effective picture of barbarian life, in that unadulterated state of which there are now so few specimens remaining. The gentleness of disposition that seems akin to the delicious climate, is shown in contrast with traits of savage fierceness;—on one page, we read of manners and modes of life that indicate a whole system of innocence and peace; and on the next, we catch a glimpse of a smoked human head, and the half-picked skeleton of what had been (in a culinary sense) a *well-dressed* man. The author's descriptions of the native girls are voluptuously colored, yet not more so than the exigencies of the subject appear to require. He has that freedom of view—it would be too harsh to call it laxity of principle—which renders him tolerant of codes of morals that may be little in accordance with our own; a spirit proper enough to a young and adventurous sailor, and which makes his book the more wholesome to our staid landsmen. The narrative is skilfully managed, and in a literary point of view, the execution of the work is worthy of the novelty and interest of its subject.

From *The Salem Advertiser* (Salem, Mass.), 25 March 1846; rpt. Randall Stewart, "Hawthorne's Contributions to *The Salem Advertiser,*" *American Literature*, 5 (January 1934), 327-41.

From *The Columbian:* 1847

WE GIVE the place of honor to the most popular of the recent issues of the press. The author of Typee, Mr. Herman Melville, has shared, to a certain extent, the good fortune of . . . Lord Byron—that of going to bed at night an unknown personage and finding himself famous when he got up the next morning. Typee has been read, we suppose, by every man, woman and child in the Union who undertakes to keep pace at all with the march of the current literature; and its fame has gone abroad also to lands beyond sea. The reliability of its narrative and descriptions is still one of the disposable questions in "literary circles;" but, whether romance or reality, all voices are unanimous in laudation of its interest and pleasantness.

Omoo differs from its elder brother in apparent credibility. Whether it is that the Society Islands are better known to the mass of readers than the Marquesas, or that Mr. Melville, in writing of the former, has thought it prudent to hold his fancy somewhat more in check, the story does not seem to draw so extensively upon the faith of the reader; in fact, so far as we have run through its pages—for our reading leisure is somewhat scant, and we have yet a third or more of Mr. Melville's story to enjoy—there is positively nothing which may not be literally true; the utmost that can be suspected, even by a jealous critic, is that the author has made the most of his materials and opportunities. About a hundred pages, for instance, are occupied by the history of a voyage from the Marquesas to Tahiti, on board a crazy old whaler, with an extremely odd assortment of a crew, every individual of which is made to sit (or stand) for his portrait; the delineations are capital, full of spirit and none the less amusing for being perhaps overdrawn; and every day of the voyage supplies its quota of incident or anecdote. Curious readers may be tempted to suggest that "little Jule" was a remarkable vessel, in being so wondrously exempt from the monotony which is generally understood to be the characteristic of whaling voyages; but this cavil is easily disposed of by the consideration that as one searching for adventures Mr. Melville is a lucky man, and farther that . . . adventure is easily found by one who has a quick eye to observe and a genial spirit to enjoy and improve. It is with travel as with matrimony—the idiosyncrasy of the party has a great deal to do with it.

The greater part of the volume is occupied by a description of, and narrative of the author's personal adventures in, the Society Islands—especially Tahiti. . . . On the whole Mr. Melville's presentation of the islands and their inhabitants, native and foreign, commends itself to the reader's understanding as worthy of full belief; but we must say that it plays sad havoc with the romance that has so long attached to the prevalent conception of this oceanic Arcadia. The excessive beauty and grace of all that nature has done of the islands are not diminished in Mr. Melville's account; but he leaves us with a much reduced estimate not only of the islanders in their original character but also in their character as converts to Christianity. Whether as Pagans or Christians they figure in his pages for the most part as a worthless, profligate and thoroughly corrupt race, for whom the missionaries seem to have done little of any real value. And they are presented not only as profligate and corrupt but, to the still more thorough destruction of all that is romantic, as ridiculous and absurd; veritable savages in character, manners and acquirements; with nothing but personal beauty to save them from being positively disgusting. We regret to say that Mr. Melville gives even a darker shade to the general impression that intercourse with civilized men has afforded to the islanders but little compensation, if any whatever, for the vices and elements of degradation by which it has been accompanied.

From *The Columbian Lady's and Gentleman's Magazine* (New York), 7 (June 1847), 283.

BAYARD TAYLOR (?): 1849

MR. MELVILLE has given us here [in *Mardi*] an acknowledged romance, and those who doubted the veracity of "Typee" and "Omoo," may now have an opportunity of noticing the difference between Mr. Melville recording what he has observed, and Mr. Melville recording what he has imagined. It appears to us that the two processes in the author's mind have little in common, and the best evidence of the truthfulness of his former books is the decidedly romantic character of much of the present.

"Mardi" is altogether the most striking work which Mr. Melville has produced, exhibiting a range of learning, a fluency of fancy, and an originality of thought and diction, of which "Typee," with all its distinctness and luxuriance of description, gave little evidence. At the same time it has defects indicating that the author has not yet reached the limits of his capacity, and that we may hope from him works better even than the present. "Mardi" is of the composite order of mental architecture, and the various rich materials which constitute it are not sufficiently harmonized to produce unity of effect. It has chapters of description, sketches of character, flashes of fanciful exaggeration, and capital audacities of satire, which are inimitable, but confusion, rather than fusion, characterizes the book as a whole. Of the two volumes the first is by far the best, but both contain abundant evidence of the richness, strength and independence of the author's mind, and are full of those magical touches which indicate original genius.

From *Graham's American Monthly Magazine of Literature and Art* (Philadelphia), 34 (June 1849), 385.

PHILARÈTE CHASLES: 1849

WE HAVE here [in *Mardi*] a curious novelty, an American Rabelais. Fancy what the prodigious Pantagruel would have been, if our Meudon *curé* had added elegiac, transparent, and pearl-like tints to the canvas of his vigorous irony, and enhanced the originality of his arabesques with Pantheistic philosophy. Fancy Daphnis and Chloe, or Paul and Virginia in the bosom of a cloud, dancing I know not what strange gavotte, with Aristotle and Spinoza, escorted by Gargantua and Gargamelle. A work such as was never before heard of, worthy of a Rabelais without gaiety, a Cervantes without grace, a Voltaire without taste. Mardi and a Voyage Thither is none the less one of the most singular books which has appeared anywhere upon the face of the globe for a long time. You might accumulate upon it all the epithets that Madame de Sevigné affectionated; an extraordinary and vulgar book, original and incoherent, full of sense and nonsense, stuffed full of interesting facts and repetition, profound instruction, and indifferent epigrams. You might call it the dream of an ill-educated cabin boy, who has intoxicated himself with hashish, and is swayed to and fro by the wind on the fore-top during a midsummer night in the tropics.

This bizarre work, commencing as a novel, turning into a fairy tale, and availing itself of allegory to reach the satirical after passing through the elegy, the drama, and the burlesque novel, piqued greatly my curiosity as a critic; I did not understand it after I had read it, I understood it still less after I had re-read it; a key was necessary not only for the comprehension of the facts, the proper names, and the doctrines which the author introduced, but above all to the composition of such a book, which appeared to have no reason in the world to be in the world. With that love of the truth and that necessity of going to the bottom of things which I neither can nor would extinguish, I set to work to solve a problem which had all the more interest as relating to an entirely new literature, which is still, so to speak, in the egg-shell. I consulted the English criticisms; they told me what I already knew—in the first place that the work was an extravagant one, and in the second, that they saw their way no more clearly than I did. They also informed me that Mr. Herman Melville was a pseudonym for the author of the apocryphal romance-voyages, Typee and Omoo, which exhibit vigorous power of imagination and great hardihood in lying.

In consequence I read Typee . . . and also Omoo . . . , and I did not agree with the English critics. They treat without doubt of a thousand strange adventures, of nymphs, lovelorn and savage, of idyllic and philosophical cannibals, of temples buried in the woods and perched on tops of the rocks of Nukuheva, of beautiful *Morais* in the villages, of innocent scenes of anthropophagism varied with sentimental dances, but pretty much these identical things are found in the pages of Bougainville, Onga, Ellis, and Earle. There was an impression of truth, a savor of an unknown and primitive nature, a vivacity of impression which struck me. The colors appeared to me to be real, although a little too warm and somewhat heightened for effect, while the romantic adventures of the author were turned off with sufficient probability. . . .

After having read Typee and Omoo, I had, as I have said, great doubt as to the justice of the opinion which had prevailed in America and in England, and which is expressed in most of the journals and reviews in which the "romances" of Mr. Melville are analysed. The freshness and profundity of the impressions reproduced in these books astonished me; I saw in their writer one less skilful in amusing himself with a dream, and in playing with a cloud, than constrained by a powerful recollection, which had gained possession of him. A type of the Anglo-American character, living for and by sensation, curious as an infant, adventurous as a savage, the first to throw himself head-foremost into unheard-of adventures, and carrying them through with desperate enthusiasm, I found that Mr. Herman Melville had there depicted himself most faithfully. . . .

[In the following issue of *The Literary World* a week later, after some preliminaries, the review continues thus:]

The real value of these two works consists, as we see, in their vivacity of impression, and lightness of touch of the pencil. Led away by his first success, the author afterwards attempted to write a new humoristic book, Mardi, and a Voyage Thither. Irritated by the false reputation for invention which had been bestowed upon him, he took the pains to merit it, he endeavored to make use of the treasures of the imagination which had been lent to him. . . .

The whole of this part of the book [the narrator and Jarl's escaping ship by whale boat and then encountering and boarding the almost deserted Malay brigantine] save the effort continually manifested by the author to be eloquent, ingenious, and original, is charming and full of life. There is much interest and vigor in the maritime scenes, such as the pictures of the calm, the storm, and above all of the capture of the abandoned brigantine. You would think that you were commencing a recital of probable or actual adventures. No such thing. Scarcely has the author entered these delicious lagunes where spring time is eternal and the night luminous as the day, when he renounces reality, and fairy land and somnambulism commence.

Behold a double bark, bearing upon one of its two prows a dais covered with flowers and precious stuffs, manned by twelve Polynesians, who appear to obey an old man with a white beard, covered with ornaments. Jarl, Melville, and two natives, put off in their boat to meet these strangers. A combat follows the encounter; the priest, who attacks Melville and his friends with fury, is mortally wounded, his acolytes take to flight, and a young girl who had been concealed on the dais, white as an European, her complexion as transparent as the pearl, her eyes blue as the iris, becomes the conquest of the invaders.

She is a white girl, some of whom are occasionally born in these regions, and is called Yillah; the priest was conducting her with great ceremony to the sacred isle, where she was to be sacrificed to the deity of evil. Melville, it is to be understood, is very much taken with Yillah, who has no recommendation but beauty; a more insignificant heroine or more fastidious divinity cannot be conceived.

As far as the somnambulism awakened by this part of the book permits the intentions of the American author to be divined, Yillah should represent "human happiness" sacrificed by the priests. Mr. Melville has an old grudge against the priesthood, and since the missionaries of the *New York Evangelist,* his dislike seems to have been envenomed.

Here commences a symbolic Odyssey of the strangest nature, very clumsily imitated from Rabelais—an odyssey which is to plunge us in a world of extravagant phantoms and allegorical shades. The adventurers visit in turn the chiefs of the small islands of the Archipelago, which have all a symbolic signification. Borabolla the gastronome evidently represents epicureanism; Maramma is the religious world, superstition; Donjalolo is the poetic world; the antiquarian Oh-Oh is the symbol of erudition. One chapter seems to be devoted to the etiquette of the Spaniards, another to the artistic genius of the Italians, a third to French mobility. I think that the island of Pimminy must be the fashionable world, the society of exquisites, of which Mr. Melville makes a sufficiently piquant satire. It is, in two words, young America amusing himself with old Europe. We would not be sorry to receive some lessons from this young infant precocious and robust; our decrepitude has need of them and we are playing very sad comedies, but Mr. Melville has taken a wrong course to indoctrinate or parody us. Of what import to us are the interminable excursions of Melville, Samoah, and Jarl? What have we to do with King Prello and King Xipho, who symbolize feudality and military glory. Those then are not our present terrors. Our nineteenth century has other enemies to combat.

At last a queen, Queen Hautia, who is smitten with the traveller, takes upon herself to abduct the young captain. From time to time Hautia, who seems to be something like voluptuousness, sends three of her *femmes de chambre* to Melville, armed with symbolic flowers, which the hero never fails to send back to her. In the midst of this chaos the old theories of D'Holbach, the already superannuated dogmas of Hegel, the pantheistic algebra of Spinoza, are mixed and pitched together in inextricable confusion. The philosophical common-places of the rationalistic schools are veiled under a thousand symbolic folds, which the author seems to consider something grand—let him know that we are completely blaséd by the blasphemies.

The second volume is devoted to this obscure satire of European faiths, and the vague doctrines of a pantheistic scepticism. None of the voyagers has been able to find human happiness (Yillah), they do not accept voluptuousness (Hautia) as sufficient compensation. They then make sail for Mardi, a kind of world in the clouds,—from metaphysical symbolism we pass to transparent allegory.

Mardi is the modern political world. This part is the most piquant of the

book. We are curious to learn how a republican of the United States judges
the civilization of the present, and resolves the obscure problem of human
destinies. Let us pass rapidly over the invention of the strange names with
which Europe, France, and America are baptized by our author: they are
Dominora (England), *Franko* (France), *Ibirie* (Spain), *Romara* (Rome), *Apsburga*
(Germany), *Kannida* (Canada). This harlequinade reminds us too much of our
own Rabelais, so fruitful in appellations, whose grotesque sound suffices to
provoke the *pantagruelian* titillation. Mr. Melville is not a magician of this kind.
He has good sense and sagacity, he would make out of them humor, which
is not the same thing.

The fantastic vessel upon which a poet, a philosopher, Mr. Melville, and
a rabble of fabulous personages of mediocre invention find themselves, touches
in turn at the shores of Europe or *Porphyro* (the morning star), and of America,
or the Land of Life (*Vivenza*). They visit Germany, England, Spain, Italy,
France. There is a filial respect and profound love in the manner in which the
author speaks of Great Britain, worthy of notice, and a thorough Anglo-Saxon
severity in the pity which he accords to Ireland. At last he sees France—the
year 1848 has just commenced.

It will be seen that our author preserves a very beautiful sang-froid in
contemplating our miseries. As soon as he sees American land, this philosophic
calm gives place to a very lively exultation.

There are few lyric chants more beautiful than this: the poet is here true
as to his proper emotion—true as to that which he expresses. In effect, what
will vast America become where each year fleets of various populations arrive
to aggregate themselves to the old puritan and calvinistic nucleus of the
Anglo-Saxon colony—what will be the genius of this new world as yet scarcely sketched? It is one of the most curious subjects for speculation and conject-
ure which can offer themselves to the philosopher. What one can affirm with
certainty is that, on the one side, America is yet very far from her necessary
development; on the other, that she will attain it in the same ratio that will
force back Europe into the shade. The Europeans are too enlightened to believe
that European civilization comprehends the past and the future of the world.
The zones of light change; the march of civilization, that of science, the
successive and constant discovery of the truth, can not only no longer be the
object of a doubt, but this vast ascendant progression is alone conformed to
the divine law and the divine love.

Mr. Melville has therefore had his eyes very wide open to the magnificent
future of his country: he predicts what will certainly arrive—the transformation
of the whole continent into an immense and renovated Europe. "It is impossible," says he, "that Canada should not become independent like the United
States: it is an event which I do not desire, but which I foresee; the thing must
come to pass. It is impossible that England should pretend to retain her power
over all the nations whom she has protected or hatched: the eternal vicissitudes
of events do not so will. The East has peopled the West, which in her turn
will repeople the East—it is the eternal flux and reflux. Who knows but that
from the shores of America, scarcely inhabited at the present day, and which

will overflow in the course of ages, fleets of young men and grey sires will go forth to regenerate Europe become a desert, her cities ruined, and her fields deserts!" Despite this patriotic ardor and boundless confidence Mr. Melville addresses to his fellow citizens, under a symbolic veil, it is true—hard truths, and good to be understood. His sermon is too remarkable for us not to translate it literally.

When Mr. Melville has visited and criticised Europe and America, he turns his course again towards the metaphysical regions, where he admires, without being able to inhabit them, the kingdoms of Alma, and the domains of Serenia. Alma represents the Saviour; Serenia is his domain. Yillah, or human happiness, is lost for ever, and Mr. Melville resigns himself to do without it.

Such is the colossal machine invented by Mr. Melville. . . .

In the midst of this puerile and fatiguing confusion, among the many faults of taste and incoherencies which shock the reader, talent and reason, as we have seen, are not wanting to this singular writer. The words which he addresses to the French deserve to be pondered.

From *The Literary World,* 4 August 1849, pp. 89-90; 11 August 1849, pp. 101-103. The New York journal was reprinting the Frenchman's criticism from the *Revue des Deux Mondes* of Paris.

From *The Athenaeum:* 1851

THIS [*The Whale,* as *Moby-Dick* was entitled in Britain] is an ill-compounded mixture of romance and matter-of-fact. The idea of a connected and collected story has obviously visited and abandoned its writer again and again in the course of composition. The style of his tale is in places disfigured by mad (rather than bad) English; and its catastrophe is hastily, weakly, and obscurely managed. The second title—'Moby Dick'—is the name given to a particular sperm whale, or white sea monster, more malignant and diabolical even than the sperm whale in general is known to be. This ocean fiend is invested with especial horrors for our ship's crew;—because, once upon a time, a conflict with him cost their Captain a limb. Captain Ahab had an ivory leg made,—took an oath of retribution,—grew crazy,—lashed himself up into a purpose of cruising in quest of his adversary,—and bound all who sailed with him to stand by him in his wrath. With this cheerful Captain, on such a wise and Christian voyage of discovery, went to sea Ishmael, the imaginary writer of this narrative.

Frantic though such an invention seems to be, it might possibly have been accepted as the motive and purpose of an *extravaganza* had its author been consistent with himself. Nay, in such a terrible cause—when Krakens and Typhoons and the wonders of Mid-Ocean, &c. &c. were the topics and toys to be arranged and manoeuvred—we might have stretched a point in admission of electrical verbs and adjectives as hoarse as the hurricane. There is a time for everything in imaginative literature;—and, according to its order, a place—for rant as well as for reserve; but the rant must be good, honest, shameless rant, without flaw or misgiving. . . . Ravings and scraps of useful knowledge flung together salad-wise make a dish in which there may be much surprise, but in which there is little savour. The real secret of this patchiness in the present case is disclosed in Mr. Melville's appendix; which contains such an assortment of curious quotations as Southey might have wrought up into a whale-chapter for the 'The Doctor,'—suggesting the idea that a substantial work on the subject may have been originally contemplated. Either Mr. Melville's purpose must have changed, or his power must have fallen short. The result is, at all events, a most provoking book,—neither so utterly extravagant as to be entirely comfortable, nor so instructively complete as to take place among documents on the subject of the Great Fish, his capabilities, his home and his capture. Our author must be henceforth numbered in the company of the incorrigibles who occasionally tantalize us with indications of genius, while they constantly summon us to endure monstrosities, carelessnesses, and other such harassing manifestations of bad taste as daring or disordered ingenuity can devise.

The opening of this wild book contains some graphic descriptions of a dreariness such as we do not remember to have met with before in marine literature. Sick of shore, Ishmael, the narrator, resolves to go to sea in a whaler; and on his way to Nantucket with that object, he is detained at New Bedford [where he meets a harpooner] . . . .

The dark-complexioned harpooner turned out to be a cannibal, one Queequeg,—as sweet-tempered a savage as if he had been a prize vegetarian. It seemed odd enough to find Miss [Harriet] Martineau in her 'Eastern Travel' professing that "she had never rested till she had mastered the religious idea involved in cannibalism,"—but Mr. Melville's impersonation of the virtues and humanities which are to light up and relieve his terrible story is yet odder as a selection. The Battas, who, as Sir Stamford Raffles assures us, eat their progenitors when the latter are sixty years old, are henceforth not beyond the reach of *rehabilitation:*—nay, those most dismal of Gnomes, the aborigines who devour clay, may now expect their laureate and their apologist. To such lengths will a craving for effect carry a sane man!

We have little more to say in reprobation or in recommendation of this absurd book,—having detailed its leading incident. Mr. Melville has been on former occasions characterized by us as one who thoroughly understands the tone of sea superstition. There is a wild humorous poetry in some of his terrors which distinguishes him from the vulgar herd of fustian-weavers. For instance, his interchapter on 'The Whiteness of the Whale' is full of ghostly suggestions for which a Maturin or a Monk Lewis would have been thankful. Mr. Melville has to thank himself only if his horrors and his heroics are flung aside by the general reader, as so much trash belonging to the worst school of Bedlam literature,—since he seems not so much unable to learn as disdainful of learning the craft of an artist.

From *The Athenaeum: Journal of Literature, Science, and the Fine Arts* (London), 25 October 1851, pp. 1112-13.

GEORGE RIPLEY (?): 1851

A NEW work by HERMAN MELVILLE, entitled *Moby Dick; or, The Whale*, has just been issued by Harper and Brothers, which, in point of richness and variety of incident, originality of conception, and splendor of description, surpasses any of the former productions of this highly successful author. *Moby Dick* is the name of an old White Whale; half fish and half devil; the terror of the Nantucket cruisers; the scourge of distant oceans; leading an invulnerable, charmed life; the subject of many grim and ghostly traditions. This huge sea monster has a conflict with one Captain Ahab; the veteran Nantucket salt comes off second best; not only loses a leg in the affray, but receives a twist in the brain; becomes the victim of a deep, cunning monomania; believes himself predestined to take a bloody revenge on his fearful enemy; pursues him with fierce demoniac energy of purpose; and at last perishes in the dreadful fight, just as he deems that he has reached the goal of his frantic passion. On this slight framework, the author has constructed a romance, a tragedy, and a natural history, not without numerous gratuitous suggestions on psychology, ethics, and theology. Beneath the whole story, the subtle, imaginative reader may perhaps find a pregnant allegory, intended to illustrate the mystery of human life. Certain it is that the rapid, pointed hints which are often thrown out, with the keenness and velocity of a harpoon, penetrate deep into the heart of things, showing that the genius of the author for moral analysis is scarcely surpassed by his wizard power of description.

In the course of the narrative the habits of the whale are fully and ably described. Frequent graphic and instructive sketches of the fishery, of sea-life in a whaling vessel, and of the manners and customs of strange nations are interspersed with excellent artistic effect among the thrilling scenes of the story. The various processes of procuring oil are explained with the minute, painstaking fidelity of a statistical record, contrasting strangely with the weird, phantom-like character of the plot, and of some of the leading personages, who present a no less unearthly appearance than the witches in Macbeth. These sudden and decided transitions form a striking feature of the volume. Difficult of management, in the highest degree, they are wrought with consummate skill. To a less gifted author, they would inevitably have proved fatal. He has not only deftly avoided their dangers, but made them an element of great power. They constantly pique the attention of the reader, keeping curiosity alive, and presenting the combined charm of surprise and alternation.

The introductory chapters of the volume, containing sketches of life in the great marts of Whalingdom, New Bedford and Nantucket, are pervaded with a fine vein of comic humor, and reveal a succession of portraitures, in which the lineaments of nature shine forth, through a good deal of perverse, intentional exaggeration. To many readers, these will prove the most interesting portions of the work. Nothing can be better than the description of the owners of the vessel, Captain Peleg and Captain Bildad, whose acquaintance we make before the commencement of the voyage. The character of Captain Ahab also opens upon us with wonderful power. He exercises a wild, bewildering fascination by his dark and mysterious nature, which is not at all diminished when we obtain a clearer insight into his strange history. Indeed, all the members of the ship's company, the three mates, Starbuck, Stubbs, and Flash, the wild, savage Gayheader, the case-hardened old blacksmith, to say nothing of the pearl of a New Zealand harpooner, the bosom friend of the narrator—all stand before us in the strongest individual relief, presenting a unique picture gallery, which every artist must despair of rivaling.

The plot becomes more intense and tragic, as it approaches toward the denouement. The malicious old Moby Dick, after long cruisings in pursuit of him, is at length discovered. He comes up to the battle, like an army with banners. He seems inspired with the same fierce, inveterate cunning with which Captain Ahab has followed the traces of his mortal foe. The fight is described in letters of blood. It is easy to foresee which will be the victor in such a contest. We need not say that the ill-omened ship is broken in fragments by the wrath of the weltering fiend. Captain Ahab becomes the prey of his intended victim. The crew perish. One alone escapes to tell the tale. Moby Dick disappears unscathed, and for aught we know, is the same "delicate monster," whose power in destroying another ship is just announced from Panama.

From *Harper's New Monthly Magazine* (New York), 4 (December 1851), 137.

From *Bentley's Miscellany:* 1852

WE ALWAYS had faith in the genius of Herman Melville, or rather, we had eyes to see it. Who could not perceive the fine things (and how thickly studded they were!) in Omoo and Typhee, and Mardi—who except those mightily critical connoisseurs who, detecting faults at a glance, proposed to discover beauties by shutting one eye, that they might direct a keener glance with the other, and by a mistake—arising haply from over-eagerness—closed both.

The foregoing remarks have been suggested by a perusal of Melville's last work, "The Whale," which is certainly one of the most remarkable books that has appeared for many years past. It is, however, a performance of which no brief, and at the same time intelligible, description can be rendered. Who, in a few sentences can supply such a summary of the mental and physical qualities of Captain Ahab, as shall distinctly present to the mind's eye of the reader that extraordinary character? The one over-mastering passion of the man—his furious hatred of the white whale, Moby Dick,—through what scenes of grandeur and of beauty that monomania impels him; to what encounters it leads—what catastrophe it precipitates; who is to tell in a score or two of lines? There are descriptions in this book of almost unrivalled force, coloured and warmed as they are, by the light and heat of a most poetical imagination, and many passages might be cited of vigorous thought, of earnest and tender sentiment, and of glowing fancy, which would at once suffice to show—contest or dispute about the matter being out of the question—that Herman Melville is a man of the truest and most original genius.

From "Literary Novelties for the Winter Season," *Bentley's Miscellany* (London), 31 (January 1852), 101-106.

GEORGE WASHINGTON PECK: 1852

A BAD BOOK! Affected in dialect, unnatural in conception, repulsive in plot, and inartistic in construction. Such is Mr. Melville's worst and latest work [*Pierre, or The Ambiguities*].

Some reputations seem to be born of accident. There are common-place men who on some fine day light, unknown to themselves, upon a popular idea, and suddenly rise on the strength of it into public favor. They stride the bubble for a little while, but at last its prismatic hues begin to fade; men see that the object of their applause has after all but an unsubstantial basis, and when at length the frail foundation bursts, they fall back into their original obscurity, unheeded and unlamented. Mr. Melville has experienced some such success. A few years back, he gave to the world a story of romantic adventure; this was untrue in its painting, coarse in its coloring, and often tedious and prolix in its descriptive passages. But there was a certain air of rude romance about it, that captivated the general public. It depicted scenes in a strange land, and dealt with all the interests that circle around men whose lives are passed in peril. Nor were appeals to the grosser instincts of humanity wanting. Naked women were scattered profusely through the pages, and the author seemed to feel that in a city where the ballet was admired, "Typee" would be successful. Mr. Melville thought he had hit the key-note to fame. His book was reprinted in all directions, and people talked about it, as much from the singularity of its title as from any intrinsic merit it possessed.

This was encouraging, and Mr. Melville evidently thought so, for he immediately issued a series of books in the same strain. Omoo, Mardi, White-Jacket, Redburn, followed one another in quick succession; and the foolish critics, too blind to perceive that the books derived their chief interest from the fact of the scenes being laid in countries little known, and that the author had no other stock in trade beyond tropical scenery and eccentric sailors, applauded to the very echo. This indiscriminating praise produced its usual effect. Mr. Melville fancied himself a genius, and the result of this sad mistake has been— "Pierre." . . .

Pierre aims at something beyond the mere records of adventure contained in Mardi and Omoo. The author, doubtless puffed up by the very false applause which some critics chose to bestow upon him, took for granted that he was a genius, and made up his mind to write a fine book; and he has succeeded in writing a fine book with a vengeance. Our experience of literature is necessarily large, but we unhesitatingly state, that from the period when the

Minerva press was in fashion, up to the present time, we never met with so turgid, pretentious, and useless a book as "Pierre." It is always an unpleasant and apparently invidious statement for a critic to make, that he can find nothing worthy of praise in a work under consideration; but in the case of Pierre we feel bound to add to the assertion the sweeping conclusion, that there we find every thing to condemn. If a repulsive, unnatural and indecent plot, a style disfigured by every paltry affectation of the worst German school, and ideas perfectly unparalleled for earnest absurdity, are deserving of condemnation, we think that our already expressed sentence upon Pierre will meet with the approval of every body who has sufficient strength of mind to read it through.

Mr. Pierre Glendinning, the hero of the book, and intended by the author to be an object of our mournful admiration, supports in the course of the story the arduous characters of a disobedient son, a dishonest lover, an incestuous brother, a cold-blooded murderer, and an unrepentant suicide. This *repertoire* is agreeably relieved by his playing the part of a madman whenever he is not engaged in doing any thing worse. . . .

Now, in this matter [Pierre's relationship to his illegitimate half sister Isabel] Mr. Melville has done a very serious thing, a thing which not even unsoundness of intellect could excuse. He might have been mad to the very pinnacle of insanity; he might have torn our poor language into tatters, and made from the shreds a harlequin suit in which to play his tricks; he might have piled up word upon word, and adjective upon adjective, until he had built a pyramid of nonsense, which should last to the admiration of all men; he might have done all this and a great deal more, and we should not have complained. But when he dares to outrage every principle of virtue; when he strikes with an impious, though, happily, weak hand, at the very foundations of society, we feel it our duty to tear off the veil with which he has thought to soften the hideous features of the idea, and warn the public against the reception of such atrocious doctrines. If Mr. Melville had reflected at all—and certainly we find in him but few traces of reflection—when he was writing this book, his better sense would perhaps have informed him that there are certain ideas so repulsive to the general mind that they themselves are not alone kept out of sight, but, by a fit ordination of society, every thing that might be supposed to even collaterally suggest them is carefully shrouded in a decorous darkness. Nor has any man the right, in his morbid craving after originality, to strip these horrors of their decent mystery. But the subject which Mr. Melville has taken upon himself to handle is one of no ordinary depravity; and however he may endeavor to gloss the idea over with a platonic polish, no matter how energetically he strives to wrap the mystery in a cloud of high-sounding but meaningless words, the main conception remains still unaltered in all its moral deformity. We trust that we have said enough on this topic. It is a subject that we would gladly not have been obliged to approach, and which we are exceedingly grieved that any gentleman pretending to the rank of a man of letters should have chosen to embody in a book. Nor can we avoid a feeling of surprise, that professedly moral and apparently respectable publishers like the Messrs. Harper should have ever consented to issue from their establishment any book containing such glaring abominations as "Pierre." . . .

We have already dismissed the immorality of Mr. Melville's book, which is as horrible in its tendency as Shelley's Cenci, without a ray of the eloquent genius that lights up the deformity of that terrible play; but we have yet another and less repulsive treat in store for the reader. Mr. Melville's style of writing in this book is probably the most extraordinary thing that an American press ever beheld. It is precisely what a raving lunatic who had read Jean Paul Richter in *a translation* might be supposed to spout under the influence of a particularly moonlight night. Word piled upon word, and syllable heaped upon syllable, until the tongue grows as bewildered as the mind and both refuse to perform their offices from sheer inability to grasp the magnitude of the absurdities. Who would have believed that in the present day a man would write the following, and another be found to publish it?

> "Now Pierre began to see mysteries interpierced with mysteries, and mysteries eluding mysteries; and began to seem to see the mere imaginariness of the so supposed solidest principle of human association. Fate had done this for them. Fate had separated brother and sister, till to each other they somehow seemed so not at all."—Page 193.

There, public! there's a style for you! There, Mr. Hawthorne, you who rely so much upon the quiet force of your language, read that and profit by it! And you, Mr. Longfellow, who love the Germans, and who in "Hyperion" have given us a sample of an ornate and poetical style, pray read it too, and tell us if it is a wise thing to bind 495 pages of such stuff together, and palm it off upon the public as a book! . . .

Perhaps one of the most remarkable features in Pierre, is the boldness of the metaphors with which it is so thickly studded. Mr. Melville's imagination stops at nothing, and clears a six-barred simile or a twenty-word antithesis with equal dexterity and daring. It is no light obstacle that will bring him up in his headlong course, and he scoffs alike at the boundaries of common sense and the limits of poetical propriety. We have just caught an image which will serve our purpose, and transfix it, butterfly-like, on our critical pin, for the admiration of scientific etymologists. It is a fine specimen, and quite perfect of its kind. Fortunately for the world, however, the species is very rare:

> "An infixing stillness now thrust a long rivet through the night, and fast nailed it to that side of the world!"—Page 219.

This is a grand and simple metaphor. To realize it thoroughly, all we have to do is to imagine some Titantic upholsterer armed with a gigantic nail, and hammer to match, hanging one hemisphere with black crape.

His description of a lady's forehead is equally grand and incomprehensible. He says, "The vivid buckler of her brow seemed as a magnetic plate." Trephining is rather an uncommon operation, but we fancy that this lady's head must have undergone some such treatment, in order to warrant her forehead being likened to a "vivid buckler."

Mr. Melville, among other improvements, has favored us with a new substantive of his own invention. We are very grateful to him for this little attention, but our thankfulness would be rendered still more willingly if he had appended a little note explaining the meaning of this—no doubt very forcible—word. At page 252 we find the following sentence: "Thy *instantaneousness* hath killed her." On a first reading of this we hurriedly came to the conclusion that "instantaneousness" must be either some very old or some very new weapon of destruction. We judged simply from the fatal results attributed to it in the sentence. Can it be possible, thought we to ourselves, that the reign of the sanguinary Colt is over? that revolvers are gone out of fashion and "instantane-ousnesses" come in? What can these new weapons be like? Have they six barrels, or are they worked by steam? . . .

We have been so far particular in pointing out Mr. Melville's faults. We have attached a certain degree of importance to each of them, from the fact that we are obliged to look upon him in the light of an experienced author, and cannot allow him that boyish license which we are always ready to grant to tyros who lose themselves for the first time amid the bewildering paths of literature. Mr. Melville has written good books, and tasted largely of success, and he ought to have known better. We regret that we are not able to temper our criticism with some unalloyed praise. . . .

We have dwelt long enough upon these "Ambiguities." We fear that if we were to continue much longer, we should become ambiguous ourselves. We have, we think, said sufficient to show our readers that Mr. Melville is a man wholly unfitted for the task of writing wholesome fictions; that he possesses none of the faculties necessary for such work; that his fancy is diseased, his morality vitiated, his style nonsensical and ungrammatical, and his characters as far removed from our sympathies as they are from nature.

Let him continue, then, if he must write, his pleasant sea and island tales. We will be always happy to hear Mr. Melville discourse about savages, but we must protest against any more Absurdities, misnamed "Ambiguities."

From *The American Whig Review* (New York), 16 (November 1852), 446-54.

W. CLARK RUSSELL: 1892

HERMAN MELVILLE, as I gather from an admirable account of this fine author by Mr. Arthur Stedman, . . . went to sea in 1841. He shipped before the mast on board a whaler and cruised continuously for eighteen months in the Pacific. He saw much ocean life, and his experiences were wild and many.. . . . Yet are Melville's pictures of the forecastle life, his representation of what goes on under the deck of that part of the ship which is thumped by the handspike of the boatswain when he echoes in thunder the order of "All hands!" marvellously and delightfully true. I will not speak of his faithful and often beautiful and often exquisite sketches of the life and scenery of the South Sea Islands, nor of his magnificent picture of Liverpool, and the descriptions of London and of English scenery in "Redburn," and the wonderful opening chapters of "Moby Dick." I link him with Dana; I place the two side by side as men of genius, but sailors first of all, and I claim, in their name, that to American literature the world owes the first, the best, and the enduring revelation of the secrets of one great side of the ocean life. . . .

Melville wrote out of his heart and out of wide and perhaps bitter experience; he enlarged our knowledge of the life of the deep by adding many descriptions to those which Dana had already given. His "South Seaman" is typical. Dana sighted her, but Melville lived in her. His books are now but little read. When he died the other day,—to my sorrow! for our correspondence had bred in me a deeper feeling than kindness and esteem,—men who could give you the names of fifty living American poets and perhaps a hundred living American novelists owned that they had never heard of Herman Melville; which simply means that to all intents and purposes the American sailor is a dead man, and the American merchant service to all intents and purposes a dead industry. Yet a famous man he was in those far days when every sea was bright with the American flag, when the cotton-white canvas shone starlike on the horizon, when the nasal laugh of the jolly Yankee tar in China found its echo in Peru. Famous he was; now he is neglected; yet his name and works will not die. He is a great figure in shadow; but the shadow is not that of oblivion.

From "A Claim for American Literature," *The North American Review* (New York), 154 (February 1892), 138-49.

Perspectives

ROBERT E. SPILLER

HERMAN MELVILLE (1819-1891) was a product of the upstate Dutch-British stock that Irving satirized in his Knickerbocker's History.... Born and raised in the city of New York, he was as much a Middle States American as it was then possible to be. Six years of youth spent in the headwaters capital of Albany confirmed his deep-rooted provincialism, and a tightly knit family life inculcated the certainties of a Calvinistic creed and an economic security. If [Herman's mother] Maria Gansevoort had been a little more flexible in her social and religious convictions or if [his father] Allan Melville had been a little less so in his world travels and manipulations of the family finances, the rebel Herman Melville might never have developed. Out of violent though probably suppressed emotional conflict at home came the will to kick against the stars. At the age of nineteen, according to his own somewhat fictionalized account, he was ready to ship for Liverpool, "as a substitute for pistol and ball," on the first copper-bottomed and fully rigged merchantman that he happened upon. This he did, and the outcast Ishmael was born in the heart of a shy and well mannered youth....

On his return, he found his family in even worse financial circumstances than when he had set out, and he was soon off again, this time to the South Seas on the whaler *Acushnet* from New Bedford. On July 9, 1842, "Richard T. Greene and Herman Melville deserted at Nukehiva," according to the crew list sworn to by the captain. Greene was the "Toby" who plunged inland on the wild Marquesan island with his adventurous companion, hoping that when the natives appeared from the tropical underbrush they would be the less cannibalistic of the two tribes who were reputed to inhabit the island in a state of constant warfare with each other. But the idyllic residence with the natives which Melville describes in his first published novel *Typee* (1846) follows only the outline of the facts. History tells of no maiden Fayaway of the canoe and the inland pool and no watchful Kory-Kory to attend the fearful but contented captive. The escapes of Toby and then of the author are attested, as is the decrepit whaler *Julia* under another name, the new companion Doctor Long Ghost (of all Melville's people, the most lovingly and ironically drawn), and the adventures in and near Tahiti, as told in the sequel *Omoo* (1847). There the chronological parallel between fiction and fact is broken. The wandering sailor, after another whaling cruise in the waters off Japan, finally enlisted in the Navy in order to ship on the man-of-war *United States* and return from Honolulu to Boston, where he was discharged on October 14, 1844.

His marriage on August 4, 1847, to the daughter of Chief Justice Lemuel Shaw transformed the world wanderer into the respectable family man and citizen. From then on, except for a few brief trips, Herman Melville could be found in New York City or at his rural home Arrowhead near Pittsfield, Massachusetts. His brief friendship with Hawthorne, who was in nearby Lenox in 1850-1851, and a trip to the Holy Land alone in 1856 are the major events of his later years in so far as his writing is concerned. The psychologist is concerned with the inner violence often caused by a life of apparent conformity; the reader is interested only in the writings that supply his imagination with the probings and insights of an aroused but suppressed genius. From 1846 to 1852 Melville wrote and published furiously; from 1853 to 1857 he continued to write, but much of his imaginative abandon had given way to critical uncertainties; from 1858 to the end of his life, a period of over thirty years, he lapsed into comparative silence and his novels were almost forgotten. . . .

From *The Cycle of American Literature: An Essay in Historical Criticism* (New York: Macmillan, 1955), pp. 91, 93-94.

NEWTON ARVIN

WITH HIS mother ... was inextricably associated what was surely the most decisive intellectual and spiritual influence of his early life, his saturation in orthodox Calvinism. It was not literally true, as he says humorously in *Moby Dick,* that he had been "born and bred in the bosom of the infallible Presbyterian Church." His Melville ancestors, to be sure, had been leaders in the Scots kirk since the days of Andrew Melville ("Scourge of Bishops") and John Knox, but Thomas Melville, his grandfather, had succumbed to the liberalizing influences of late eighteenth-century Boston and turned Unitarian. It was in the spiritual domain of Buckminster and Channing that Allan Melville had been reared, and his own religious outlook, as a result, was a typically Unitarian fusion of reasonableness, optimism, "Arminianism," and trust in the rational beneficence of a paternal deity; a kind of pious Deism, in short, with belated overtones of the *Essay on Man.* These are the tones one hears when, in a letter to his brother-in-law, Allan speaks of a God "who sees the end from the beginning, & reconciles partial evil with universal good." Perhaps, even in early childhood, Allan's second son might have caught from him something of this liberal and enlightened theological cheerfulness; if so, it would have helped to engender some of the spiritual conflicts from which he was certainly to suffer.

For Unitarianism was, almost by definition, a cool and unaggressive theology, and Allan Melville seems not to have insisted on his own bias in the religious rearing of the children. It was Maria Melville's inherited Calvinism that took the primacy here. It was in a Dutch Reformed Church that perhaps all the children, certainly Herman, were baptized; it was the Broome Street Church (Dutch Reformed) that they all attended during most of their New York years; and in the first melancholy days of her bereavement it was a Reformed church, the ancient North Church in Albany, that Maria took at last the formal step of "joining." It would have been the soundest, most conservative Calvinist orthodoxy that Melville in his teens imbibed from the sermons of the Rev. Mr. Ludlow or the Rev. Mr. Vermilye, successive pastors of that church.

Neither the humanitarian rationalism of the Enlightenment nor the transcendental, romantic ardors of the early nineteenth century had availed in any way to soften or emasculate the austere, earnest, pessimistic orthodoxy of the Reformed Church in America. Still, in Melville's childhood, its standards of doctrine, unweakened since the sixteenth century, continued to be the old

Belgic Confession, the Heidelberg Catechism, the famous Canons of the Synod of Dort. Melville need not as a boy have mastered these rigorous formulations of doctrine in order to be deeply affected by the teaching and preaching that flowed from them, to have his sense of man and the universe profoundly, however indirectly, molded by them. The whole tendency of Reformed doctrine, as a writer on the Church once said, was "to exalt God and abase man"; and the future author of *Moby Dick* was not likely to listen light-mindedly to such a gospel. A God whose sovereignty was absolute and whose power was infinite; a just, rigorous, angry, but also merciful God, whose ways were not to be searched or sounded by mortal understanding—such was the deity that, as everyone knows, Calvinism had imagined and evoked from the beginning. A deity, moreover, who had foreknown and forewilled all possible events in universal or human life, and by whom all things were determined. "We believe," says the Belgic Confession, "that the same God, after he created all things, did not forsake them, or give them up to fortune or chance, but that he rules and governs them according to his holy will, so that nothing happens in this world without his appointment." A transcendent Father, in short, whose anger one might well fear but whose goodness and justice, inscrutable though they were, one might not question. A Father whose lineaments might have been descried by the young Melville in the stanzas of an old Reformed hymn, a hymn of the sort he was himself to imitate:

> Can creatures, to perfection, find
> Th'eternal, uncreated mind?
> Or can the largest stretch of thought
> Measure and search his nature out?

.   .   .   .   .

> He frowns, and darkness veils the moon,
> The fainting sun grows dim at noon;
> The pillars of heav'n's starry roof
> Tremble and start at his reproof.

> These are a portion of his ways;
> But who shall dare describe his face?
> Who can endure his light, or stand
> To hear the thunders of his hand?

Of the children of this perfect Father, however—of humankind—what could be said except that, in Adam, they had one and all sinned against their Father and disobeyed him, and that they were, in consequence, as natural men, sunk in the most wretched condition of utter and absolute depravity? "Therefore all men," read the Canons of the Synod of Dort, "are conceived in sin, and are by nature children of wrath, incapable of any saving good, prone to evil, dead in sin, and in bondage thereto." From within man's own fallen nature, in the darkness of his corrupted will, no hope of salvation can imaginably arise. Such is the somber view of the human condition that would have been inculcated in Melville at home, at church, even at school, in his early years. Such is the view which he himself later described as "that Calvinistic sense of Innate Depravity and Original Sin, from whose visitations, in some shape or other, no deeply thinking mind is always and wholly free." The just penalty for this depravity, as he well knew, was eternal and irretrievable damnation for most of mankind; but he knew too that, according to orthodoxy, God had willed, out of his infinite mercy and inexplicable goodness, to elect a small number of human souls to salvation and eternal beatitude. For this they had to thank, not their own merits, which were nonexistent, but the free grace of God, unmerited but "irresistible." What is mere human goodness or virtue but the "filthy rags" of our righteousnesses? God's arbitrary grace is all; and it was in this spirit that Melville himself was once to allude to "that most true Christian doctrine of the utter nothingness of good works."

Of course one ought not to overstate or falsely simplify. In the prevailingly cheerful, democratic, "progressive" America of the 'twenties and 'thirties, far too many other currents of thought were moving for Melville to be obsessively and inescapably overshadowed by a sixteenth- or even a nineteenth-century Calvinism. Yet the religious tone of his mother's household seems to have become increasingly intense as time passed; one hears of formal family prayers, of the reading of religious tracts, of a somber observance of the Sabbath. And Melville's mature mind is incomprehensible save partly against this dark-hued distance. In some important senses, given the kind of imaginative writer he was by nature, this youthful indoctrination was a fortunate and positive thing. Better that his mind should have been imbrued in the severe grandeurs of Calvinist pessimism than in the "icehouse" chill of Unitarian complacency. Against the shock of discovering what devils his fellow-men could become, of encountering in his own experience "the mystery of iniquity," Melville was at least partly braced by the doctrines he had heard expounded in the North Church. Braced, too, against the discovery of the terrible limits imposed upon human will and desire by the tough, unmalleable, implacable resistance in things; by Necessity, if one chooses to call it that, by Fate, by God's will; in any case, by some force or forces in experience that "determine" or "predestine" what shall befall us, and not our purposes. Besides, there was always present at the heart of Calvinist Protestantism, despite its dogmatisms, that essentially humble and saving sense of something unaccountable, something unanalyzable and incomprehensible, something mysterious in the scheme of things, in "God's ways," that was to find so deeply responsive an echo in Melville's own meditations.

From *Herman Melville* (New York: William Sloane, 1950), pp. 30-34.

VERNON LOUIS PARRINGTON

THE VOLCANIC passions pent up in Herman Melville's heart, the ardent imagination that sent him forth on long quests and brought him home empty-handed, can scarcely be traced to any source in Maria Gansevoort or Allan Melville. A strange, incomprehensible child he seemed to his mother, and strange and incomprehensible he remained in the eyes of the family—an ugly duckling of another breed than theirs. A bitter sense of aloofness and alienation from the intimacies of family sympathy seems early to have taken possession of him, and he felt himself quietly thrust out of the circle of respectable contacts. Melville's writings are filled with thinly veiled autobiography, and it is a careless reader who does not see in *Pierre* and *Moby Dick* confessions as frank as Rousseau's. "Call me Ishmael," is the opening injunction of the latter. . . . An Ishmael Melville unhappily conceived himself to be, an outcast and wanderer on the earth because man is an outcast and wanderer, to whom Nirvana is the only comfort and hope; and when he returned disillusioned from the South Seas, when he found no home by his own fireside, when he discovered his transcendental craftsmanship driving on the rocks of economic necessity, when the public rejected his mystical dreams and he was inexorably "damned by dollars," he perforce turned in upon his own broodings and sought solace in Plato. Driven by need from his hill farm in the Berkshires, he buried himself in the "Babylonish brick-kiln of New York," to pass long years pottering about the customhouse. It was the vast futility of life as he experienced it, that sent him to his study to find there such compensation as he might.

The stages in Melville's progress towards Nirvana are sufficiently marked by the four books, *Typee, Mardi, Moby Dick,* and *Pierre.* . . .

Like all the transcendentalists Melville was a democrat, but his democracy sprang rather from his sympathies than from his philosophy. It was a democracy learned rather from Ecclesiastes than from Emerson; it sprang from his pessimism rather than from any transcendental faith in the divinity of man. He knew only too well how weak and foolish are the children of Adam; but in presence of the common fate to which the indifferent years hurry us, how stupid and callous are the social distinctions that society erects! Why should not life be a leveler, as well as death? His experience before the mast had taught him sympathy for the common man; he regarded quizzically the ways of the exploiting few and the sufferings of the exploited many; and he smiled ironically at the neat little classification that divides the human animal into sinners and saints. He was as comprehensive a democrat as Whitman, of the same all-embracing school that denied the common social and ethical categories of excellence; but alienated from his fellows, not drawn to them as Whitman was. It was not a sense of social aloofness that held him apart, but the isolation of loneliness. . . .

Such a man would not so much turn critic as embody criticism. His life— even more than Emerson's—laid upon America, was a yardstick to measure the shortcomings of a professed civilization. Cooper was a critic whom America could understand, and America hated him for his unpleasant frankness. Melville it could not understand, and it turned away and ignored him. Perhaps it was well enough that his generation could not comprehend his devastating speculations, and called him mad; or it would have cried out to crucify this maligner of all the tribal fetishes. He would level every barrier against the unpleasant that his age was erecting. He outran Thoreau in contempt for current material ideals. To turn scornfully away from the triumphs of his fellows—from the fruits of the industrial revolution and the romantic gospel of progress—this was incomprehensible blasphemy! Yet what had Herman Melville in common with middle-class America? Its hopes and fears were not his. He was troubled about life, and not about things. . . .

From *Main Currents in American Thought, Vol. II: The Romantic Revolution in America* (New York: Harcourt, Brace, 1927), pp. 261, 265-66.

D. H. LAWRENCE

THE GREATEST seer and poet of the sea for me is Melville. His vision is more real than Swinburne's, because he doesn't personify the sea, and far sounder than Joseph Conrad's, because Melville doesn't sentimentalize the ocean and the sea's unfortunates. . . .

Melville has the strange, uncanny magic of sea-creatures, and some of their repulsiveness. He isn't quite a land animal. There is something slithery about him. Something always half-seas-over. In his life they said he was mad—or crazy. He was neither mad nor crazy. But he was over the border. He was half a water animal, like those terrible yellow-bearded Vikings who broke out of the waves in beaked ships. . . .

Melville is like a Viking going home to the sea, encumbered with age and memories, and a sort of accomplished despair, almost madness. For he cannot accept humanity. He can't belong to humanity. Cannot. . . .

Never man instinctly hated human life, our human life, as we have it, more than Melville did. And never was a man so passionately filled with the sense of vastness and mystery of life which is non-human. He was mad to look over our horizons. Anywhere, anywhere out of *our* world. To get away. To get away, out! . . .

Melville hated the world: was born hating it. But he was looking for heaven. That is, choosingly. Choosingly, he was looking for paradise. Unchoosingly, he was mad with hatred of the world. . . .

Melville at his best invariably wrote from a sort of dream-self, so that events which he relates as actual fact have indeed a far deeper reference to his own soul, his own inner life.

So in *Typee* when he tells of his entry into the valley of the dread cannibals of Nukuheva. Down this narrow, steep, horrible dark gorge he slides and struggles as we struggle in a dream, or in the act of birth, to emerge in the green Eden of the Golden Age, the valley of the cannibal savages. This is a bit of birth-myth, or re-birth myth, on Melville's part—unconscious, no doubt, because his running underconsciousness was always mystical and symbolical. He wasn't aware that he was being mystical.

From *Studies in Classic American Literature* (1923; rpt. New York: Viking, 1930), pp. 193, 194, 197, 198-99.

F. O. MATTHIESSEN

[Melville's] acquaintance with the seventeenth century dated back as early as the first piece of his work that we have, for the opening lines of 'Fragments from a Writing-Desk,' which he wrote at nineteen, contain an offhand mention of 'old Burton' [author of *The Anatomy of Melancholy*,1621]. But the bulk of Melville's reading came in the reverse sequence from that of most writers: it followed rather than preceded his experience of the world. It did not result from any formal training, for a whale ship was his Yale College and his Harvard. And only when, at twenty-five, he had come back from his wandering, could he turn to books with his whole attention, partly in the hope of finding answers to questions of belief that had absorbed him in endless hours at sea, partly with the huge gusto of the man who feels that he has long been starved of his rightful fare. His account of 'A Man-of-War Library' in *White Jacket* suggests the books that appealed to him most as he began his return to civilization: among its chance miscellany that ranged from Plutarch's *Lives* to Blair's *Rhetoric*, his enthusiasm was greatest for 'some odd volumes of plays, each of which was a precious casket of jewels of good things,' *The Jew of Malta, Old Fortunatus, The City Madam, Volpone*, and *The Alchemist. . . .*

But Browne's effect upon him had been far more manifold. Indeed, in the extraordinary transformation of Melville's aims from the two straightforward accounts of his adventures in *Typee* and *Omoo*, to the philosophic ambitions of *Mardi*, Browne's speculations operated as one of the strongest agents. Melville had been making constant use of his friend Evert Duyckinck's library, whose more than sixteen thousand volumes—one of the best private collections of the day—provided an incalculable stimulus to the growth of Melville's catholic tastes. Evert wrote to his brother George in the spring of 1848, 'By the way Melville reads Old Books. He has borrowed Sir Thomas Browne of me and says finely of the speculations of the *Religio Medici* that Browne is a kind of "crack'd Archangel." Was ever anything of this sort said before by a sailor?'

A year later, near the beginning of his new voyage in *Mardi*, Melville announced, while reflecting on the wonders of the sea still unrecorded by naturalists: 'Be Sir Thomas Brown [*sic*] our ensample; who, while exploding *Vulgar Errors*, heartily hugged all the mysteries in the Pentateuch.' He followed that example to the farthest reach. . . . The books that really spoke to Melville became an immediate part of him to a degree hardly matched by any other of our great writers in their maturity. His first intense response to Browne went to the length of ventriloquism. It was hardly Melville's own voice that spoke in these wide-sweeping images of space and time: 'We glided on for hours in twilight; when, on those mountains' farther side, the hunters must have been abroad, morning glories all astir'; or, 'What shaft has yet been sunk to the antipodes? what underlieth the gold mines?' The chief reason why Melville re-echoed the music of some of Browne's very phrases was that here he had found an author who spoke to him of the 'wingy Mysteries in Divinity,' who spoke to his own awakening sense of the complexity of truth, of the difficulty of faith, since, as Browne said, 'God hath not made a Creature that can comprehend him.' The necessity to come to a reckoning with such problems became severe for Melville, as it could not be for the transcendentalists, whose serene affirmations were never tested by as much suffering and evil as he had seen. He could not avoid squaring faith with experience. . . .

Melville did not achieve in *Moby-Dick* a *Paradise Lost* or a *Faust*. The search for the meaning of life that could be symbolized through the struggle between Ahab and the White Whale was neither so lucid nor so universal. But he did apprehend therein the tragedy of extreme individualism, the disasters of the selfish will, the agony of a spirit so walled within itself that it seemed cut off from any possibility of salvation. Beyond that, his theme of the White Whale was so ambivalent that as he probed into the meaning of good and evil he found their expected values shifting. His symbols were most comprehensive when they enabled him to elicit 'what remains primeval in our formalized humanity,' when they took such a basic pattern as that of his later discernment [in *Billy Budd*] of Abraham and Isaac in Captain Vere and Billy. When the Pacific called out the response of his united body and mind, he wrote the enduring signature of his age. He gave full expression to its abundance, to its energetic desire to master history by repossessing all the resources of the hidden past in a timeless and heroic present. But he did not avoid the darkness in that past, the perpetual suffering in the heart of man, the broken arc of his career which inevitably ends in death. He thus fulfilled what Coleridge held to be the major function of the artist: he brought 'the whole soul of man into activity.'

From *American Renaissance: Art and Expression in the Age of Emerson and Whitman* (New York: Oxford Univ. Press, 1941), pp. 121-23, 656.

LAWRANCE THOMPSON

THE TYPICAL Reformation riddle-answer [to the question of man's relation to God] was that man could achieve his ultimate salvation and atonement only through abject and self-effacing bondage to God; through strait obedience to the laws of God, as revealed in the Bible. By contrast, the ancient pagan contention which returned to popularity during the Renaissance was that man could achieve his ultimate self-realization and fulfillment as a "natural man," through the liberating assertion of his own natural powers of body and mind and spirit, without any necessary reference to supernatural powers. Although these opposed views were subjected to endless permutations, and were sometimes formulated in combination with each other, before and during and after the sixteenth century, these answers (in their pure forms) were poles apart because one emphasized the supreme sovereignty of God, while the other emphasized the supreme sovereignty of natural man.

In his youth, Melville inherited the Reformation dogma of John Calvin, in a quite undiluted form. His devout and pious parents were members of the Dutch Reformed Church in America, and they taught their son to believe that God had created him innately depraved and predestinately damned to eternal Hell; but that he might possibly be saved from such damnation, through divine grace, if he threw himself submissively and abjectly on the mercy of God, as revealed through Jesus Christ.

Until he left home, at the age of eighteen, Melville seems to have developed a deeply-rooted belief in the essential truth of his religious heritage. Although disappointments and disillusionments began to accumulate, during his first sea voyage, and although these disillusionments increased ominously during his later voyages, Melville did not completely rebel against his Calvinistic heritage until after he had written and published his first two travel-narratives, *Typee* and *Omoo.* Even during his writing of *Mardi,* when the struggle between his beliefs and his doubts reached a crisis, he still managed to salvage a modified assertion of mystical religious affirmation, short-lived, because it did not satisfy and sustain him.

Disillusionment with one's inherited (and therefore second-hand) religious beliefs is such a familiar phase of human growth that one might suppose Melville could have worked out his own religious readjustments without carrying into later life any ineffaceable scars; that his own personal and first-hand religious experience might have modified his inherited beliefs until he could have arrived at some concept of God more acceptable and congenial to his temperament. By contrast, one might fear that Melville's concept of the Calvinistic God might gradually have become so repulsive that he might have moved through doubt and skepticism to a denial of the existence of God. This final step he never took. As it happened, however, Melville actually experimented with several different kinds of resolution, without achieving any.lasting comfort of consolation. Mystically inclined, he preferred or wanted to think of God as that benevolent and personal source of Truth, to whom each individual could talk directly; and this attitude was an important part of his Protestant heritage. Nevertheless, while writing *Mardi,* he seemed to toy with the wavering and unpleasant suspicion that God could not possibly be what Melville wanted him to be. As a result, the asserted affirmation in the tableau-conclusion of *Mardi* was merely an assertion: it lacked conviction.

Increasingly embittered by a conjunction of unfortunate experiences, immediately during and after the writing of *Mardi,* Melville arrived at a highly ironic conclusion: believing more firmly than ever in the God of John Calvin, he began to resent and hate the attributes of God, particularly the seemingly tyrannous harshness and cruelty and malice of God. Thus, instead of losing faith in his Calvinistic God, Melville made a scapegoat of him, and blamed God for having caused so many human beings to rebel. In this sense, then, we might say that Melville became an inverted mystic as soon as he began to be angry with God for being the harsh and logical punisher that the Calvinists said he was. Still influenced by the Calvinistic dogma that God did indeed try to exact from mankind a rigid letter-of-the-law obedience, and that Adam's fall was indeed the first indication of the unjust ruthlessness of God's punishment, Melville came to view God as the source from whom all evils flow, in short, the "Original Sinner," divinely depraved. But this riddle-answer was no more consoling to Melville than any of the others which he had explored, and at times during his life he continued to investigate the validity of other possible answers. Nevertheless, his inverted mysticism became a fixed idea, an obsession, which persisted during most of his life. . . .

I am interested in Melville's spiritual idiom primarily because it controlled and determined his artistic idiom. The tensions of Melville's peculiar and inverted religious beliefs prompted him to give them outlet in some kind of literary expression, and yet he hesitated to express himself frankly. He knew very well that his contemporary reading public was too deeply committed to Christian beliefs in the goodness of God to tolerate any open assertions as to the malice and evil of God. He also knew that if he should announce that he had declared his independence from the sovereignty of God, and that he had declared war against God in order to fight for his own freedom as a natural man, his Christian readers would tell him that he was being ridiculous; that it takes two to make a quarrel, and that God is above quarreling with a human being.

Still craving the satisfaction of giving literary vent to his secret and heretical beliefs, Melville gradually formulated a complex variety of stylistic and structural methods for expressing himself in such a way as to protect himself from heresy hunters. The two distinct elements with which he could experiment, in his narratives, were the stories he chose to tell, and the way in which he chose to tell them. The plots of his novels were frequently selected to represent, in vivid and dramatic pictures, his so-called heretical and blasphemous views. The way in which he chose to present these plots was not uniform; but he ingeniously arranged to pretend, in the telling, that no matter how much he indulged in occasional religious doubts and questionings, his ultimate goal was to praise and honor the orthodox Christian viewpoint. This pretense was very convenient for purposes of sarcasm and satire and irony, because the pretense gave the illusion of proceeding in a direction exactly opposite from the anti-Christian direction of the story itself, the plot itself. Within this flexible formula of sustained irony, Melville achieved ample elbowroom for playing with innumerable artistic devices for defensive concealment, subterfuge, deception, hoodwinking, ridicule.

From *Melville's Quarrel with God* (Princeton: Princeton Univ. Press, 1952), pp. 4-7.

MILTON R. STERN

IT IS axiomatic that transcendental thought is essentially ethical. The same is true of the transcendental symbol. Its purpose is moral because its basic assumption is the Ideal, and it attempts to connect history with the absolute moral order of cosmic idealism. Given the task he had set for himself, the truly romantic transcendentalist had to make symbolism his literary vehicle. The naturalist's job is more difficult, for the symbol's basic assumption is lost. Instead of being able to deduce a moral order from the Ideal, the naturalist has to create one. Paradoxically, with absolute morality gone, man's relative moralities become even more important, for there is no controlling moral symbol for the cosmos. The naturalist's task does not become one of creating new symbolic functions but rather one of creating new symbolic relationships for every chapter of man's history. This is the basic difference between Ahab's demonism and Melville's. Ahab sought the symbol because, like Lucifer, he sought to challenge the absolute. Melville, also rebelling (not against God, but against a false concept of God), sought the symbol which would allow him to replace a vacuum with relative, human demands. The entire thematic center shifts, for unlike Ahab, Melville immediately becomes earth-oriented rather than heaven-oriented; thus his "unchristian" demonism consists in his seeing the idealistic Ahab as diabolic. . . . The Melville-devil rebels against the assumptions of idealistic symbolization. He too dives to the pre-Cambrian depths of the past, and returns—but with a different message of creation. Because he was the first major American author to turn the symbology already created by the transcendentalists to the relativistic purposes of naturalism, Melville becomes the historical and artistic focal point for one of the two main branches of American literary thought.

Ahab typifies idealistic symbolic thought. It is true that to Ahab the ideal was an evil enemy of man rather than a benevolent perfection. But what is central is that he was an idealist. It is not pertinent that he would conquer the ideal rather than yieldingly merge with it. Indeed, Ahab found the most freezing terror in the thought that there might be no ideal to fight. Though he worshipped satanically like Fedallah rather than conventionally like Starbuck or hopefully like Emerson and Thoreau, he too feverishly sought God and sought to believe in God. It makes no difference how man defines what he considers to be absolute; the error is that he thinks he perceives it at all beyond the infinity of a natural existence which in itself does not have constant (by human standards) moral qualities.

But it cannot be argued that in selecting the demonized Ahab, who believing in an ideal that frustrated and limited man, Melville was stacking the deck against the idealist. For there is always Pierre, who takes action armed with a belief in the ideal as perfect Virtue, perfect Truth. There is always the Confidence Man, who tries and tries to sell his idealistic stock of faith in a benevolent and curative ideal to others. He also tries to secure faith impregnably for himself before opponents armed with experience in the countless adverse indications of history. There is always Clarel, who tries to reconcile the disparities between his own history and the assumptions which a pilgrimage to the Holy Land requires.

All these seekers and their defeats illuminate Melville's view of the quest for the Holy Grail. Melville takes as a central character the individual who makes a philosophical voyage, which is symbolized by a physical journey. The spiritual voyage is a search for the primitivist's paradisiac world, as presented in *Typee* and only incidentally in the picaresque *Omoo*. Or it is a search for the ideal's absolute perfection, as presented in *Mardi*. Sometimes it is a search for an ideal past and an absolute identity, as presented in *Redburn* and *White-Jacket*. Characteristically it is a search for ultimate truth and being, a final triumph for man's cosmic status, as presented in *Moby-Dick*. Occasionally it is a search for the possibility of behavior according to the ideal responses of the human heart, as presented in *Pierre*. And it is also a search for idealistic faith and faith's confidence as presented in *The Confidence Man* and *Clarel*. Despite arbitrary divisions, the books all share each other's problems. The richest books embrace all the problems. The totality of the books presents man's search for an informing ideal that is more than physical causation. Idealists all, the characters search for a causality that is more than something merely external to man's moral sphere.

And Melville always presents the quest as futile.

Unlike the scientists and Chillingworths of the idealist, Hawthorne, Melville's visionary villains are not materialists. Ahab's famous curse upon science indicates the idealist who projects self upon universe and replaces the facts of the material world with his own ideal, which thereby becomes the unarmed vision of monomania. "As if you can kill time without killing Eternity," says Thoreau in *Walden*. "As if you can fashion a harpoon that will kill a zero," answers Melville in all his books. He devotes the totality of his books to piling up disparities between Eternal self and Vision on the one hand and time's history of man (or should it be man's history of time) on the other. Finally the seeker, like Pierre, realizes—when he is allowed to realize—that absolute Vice and Virtue are two shadows cast by the same nothing, and that the seeker of the absolute becomes the fool of the absolute. Be they heroic or pathetic, noble or ludicrous, Melville's idealists are all finally fools. It is the fool quality that is at bottom of the circular, grim jest referred to in Melville's "metaphysical" novels—the deadly-funny joke that man makes the universe play upon himself. . . .

Beginning with *Typee,* Melville explored the conduct of wrongly informed vision. *Typee* almost certainly is not the same consciously symbolic construct that the later books are, but in this very first book there is an order sheet for the materials Melville is to use characteristically. There are the quester, the lure, the two worlds. Larger considerations of ideal and man's relationship to it do not really enter yet, but the general patterns of imagery with which such relationships will be created are introduced. Use of color, the primitive and the western, description of the human body, height, depth, land, sea, as symbolic imagery, are all here. Moreover, *Typee* sets a constant for the relationships between the four basic characters. Throughout the other books the specific patterns of imagery which present the relationships may change, but the relationships themselves do not.

In *Typee,* Tommo, the embryo quester, is exposed to the horror of primitive mindlessness, and he learns his lesson of cultural relativism. But the devil-quester that remains in Melville is yet to be exorcised. For we come to *Mardi.* *Mardi* is the central book in a study of Melville's thematic development, and it is the least unified of all the works. Still exploiting the South Seas setting (the popular success of *Typee* and *Omoo* simply amazed and delighted Melville), *Mardi* places a western story in costume. The central characters are not mindless primitives but western men, as the geographical allegory alone makes plain. Picking up character-relationships and patterns of imagery where *Typee* left off, *Mardi* is Melville's first determined attempt to tell the story of quest as a symbolic history of civilization.

Moby-Dick is the same story given artistic form and completion. Though it is the best book Melville wrote, it is not included in this study because it demonstrates the focus rather than the development of Melville's theme. But it was expanded in new directions in *Pierre,* a less satisfactory book. In *Pierre* Melville anatomized the would-be redeemer-quester who brings the primitive characteristics of pure, childlike heart to bear upon the western world into which he emerges. It is for good reason that Saddle Meadows, the estate wherein Pierre grows to young manhood, is presented as a bit of primitive Typee set in the west. It is for good reason that Pierre so often is referred to as a sleep-filled child of magnificent physique and paltry experience. The "common sense" instrumentalist cast of light that plays on this book becomes evident in the reflection that Pierre's tactical defeat is one with his metaphysical defeat. And this redeemer-quester goes through all the steps of withdrawal, deceit, a sterile relationship, murder, and suicide. The redeemer-quester, spurned by the world, becomes the hater-quester, the destroyer. *Pierre* demonstrates how Christ turns into Satan. Actually, Pierre is a more comprehensive protagonist than Ahab. Pierre goes from love to hate. We see Ahab only after he has spit on the altar, only after Christ and Satan have merged. Finding no other-world, Pierre becomes neutral, a zero like the thing he has pursued. Now Melville can allow the quester to state the thematic conclusion—ideals in any form are shadows cast by a nothing, and the champion of the ideal becomes the fool of the ideal. Pierre is carried to a realization of his untenable position once world and time are rejected. Ahab is never educated, and despite his moments of softening and doubt, he never changes. But with Pierre's death, the story of the quester is complete. What remained now for Melville was to create a hero.

What would happen if there were a man who did manage to understand the proper relationship between heart and mind, a man who was not blind to history, a man who had a political or social position—say a ship's captaincy—which would allow him to translate his realizations into action? What if this man were exposed to a choice between pure ideal and "fallen" human history, with its present actuality of a crime-filled man-of-war world? Wanted: a hero.

Captain Vere is the man created to fill this position.

Billy Budd, like the early Pierre, is pictured as the childlike barbarian, the pure creature whose only experience really is just the experience of his own inner purity and ideality. His spontaneous responses preclude control by mind. This Christ figure also deceives by silence, albeit unwittingly, and finally becomes a murderer and a causer of his own death. Billy himself is the lure which Vere painfully rejects with all the insight created by an understanding of human history. Vere is educated, with the reader, to see Claggart as Satan and Baby Budd as Christ. But Vere's one overriding fact is the fact of the temporal world, the reality of his human community to which he owes his primary allegiance. He cannot choose the ideal which, by itself, is beautiful. And Claggart becomes the other facet of Budd. Budd is the ideal, Claggart is the consequence. He is the completely mad and satanized quester who has withdrawn from quest. He is Ahab, retired in his New Bedford home, staring silently and crazily out at the sea. He is Ahab who has given up the chase, but who still watches. . . . This demonized isolato seeks out and hates and yearns to believe in ideal Billy in exactly the same monomaniacal relationship which Ahab has to the white whale. Just as the reader sees that for Ahab the whale is only what Ahab thinks he is, and the whale, in a sense, becomes Ahab, so for Melville, Christ and Satan are ultimately one entity with a dual face. Like all Melvillean dualities, absolute identities are man-made products which unite in the flow of historical consequence in the Great God Time. The bright and the dark are the *same*.

Vere rejects both lure and quester. His heartbroken rejection of Budd as a beautiful impossibility in favor of an ugly reality, his decision to force his position of command to operate according to what his head dictates and his heart detests, is his acceptance of this world as the only possible one. It is not, as many critics have attempted to demonstrate, an acceptance of God and a submission to Fate. It is quite the opposite. It is Melville's reluctant, modified, but final acceptance of historical necessity in a naturalistic universe. It is a consequent call for man to control his fate by controlling his actions in the historical world—and it is also Melville's statement of inability to find the way to do so. Vere decides to remain unwithdrawn, to accept the responsibility of the human community by accepting the responsibility of command. His decision to maintain order because of man's blindness is his sacrifice of self to the necessities of moral responsibility historically defined. Moreover, it is in his sacrifice of individual self to his social self that Vere finds his greatest identity, in the book as well as in the reader's mind. Vere is the polar opposite and instinctive antagonist to the quester. He offers the alternative behavior which had to be created once the quester's behavior was anatomized and rejected.

In *Billy Budd* the cast of characters changes. The quester as such drops out and the hero takes his place. And here the limitations (or perhaps the accuracy) of Melville's nineteenth-century naturalism become most apparent. For even the hero does not create a purged world. The lesson of Vere's sacrifice is lost. The lesson of Billy Budd's final realization is lost. The world gains not social insight but myth, and the cycle continues. . . .

From *The Fine Hammered Steel of Herman Melville* (Urbana: Univ. of Illinois Press, 1957), pp. 9-11, 25-27.

H. BRUCE FRANKLIN

MELVILLE'S MAJOR works, taken together, provide a coherent and extremely valuable exploration of myth. Like any other study of mythology, they examine and compare particular myths of the world, theorize about the mythmaking process, and ask what meanings, dangers, and values reside in myth. But they do some things which no formal study of mythology can do: they use some of the world's myths as means of ordering and defining action; they dramatize the mythmaking process in action; they dramatically display the meanings, dangers, and values of myth by showing myth itself in action.

At first Melville's mythology differed very little from that found in contemporaneous travel books. The two semi-autobiographical South Sea adventure stories use rather conventional, although unorthodox, formulas to explore the relations between Western, civilized, Christian myths and values and Polynesian, primitive, pagan myths and values. The transmutation of the raw materials began in *Mardi,* his first major work.

Mardi not only compares many of the world's myths, but also portrays the institutions, poetry, philosophy, and theology of the world as a collection of Polynesian myths. By dramatizing contemporaneous theories of mythmaking, *Mardi* tries to discover what myth means. By dramatizing the products of myth, *Mardi* tries to show what myths can do. Central to all the Mardian myths are the various myths of the savior. *Mardi* portrays all savior myths, whether embodied by the Hindu "Brami," the Incan "Manko," or the Christian "Alma," as dangerous deceptions. But it also sees in the teachings of these saviors—stripped of their dangerous mythic trappings—a possible salvation. Yet the safety of nonmythic religion of the heart cannot keep the would-be god Taji from his suicidal romantic quest.

Moby-Dick drops the Polynesian metaphor and consummates much that began in *Mardi.* Like *Mardi,* it discusses, compares, evaluates, and parodies particular myths of the world and dramatizes the mythmaking process. *Moby-Dick* also appropriates one of the world's myths—the struggle between Osiris and Typhon—to arrange its own action and reveal much of what that action means. The would-be god in *Moby-Dick* is not, like Taji, a runaway sailor chasing a pretty girl. He pursues a real, unbelievably large and destructive dragon, which represents to him what the dragon has represented to many of the nations of the world. *Moby-Dick* presents the Egyptian myth of the savior and the Leviathan he hunts as a prototype or source of many myths, and suggests itself as a more accurate version of all these myths. Osiris and Typhon represent a kind of mythical truth transcended only by the mythical truth which Ahab represents. The myth of the savior, dramatized in terms of the Egyptian and Nantucket hunter of the great demon, becomes as glorious as it is dangerous. In his dragon hunt, Ahab becomes as a god and perishes because he is not a god.

In *Pierre* comparative mythology becomes of less importance, while the ethical values of myth become more important. The narrator of *Mardi* had assumed the name of a god at first merely to protect himself in Polynesia (just like Captain Cook). Ahab had played act by act the role of a god in a godlike but ungodly madness. Both sacrificed everything to their search for the divine. Pierre, however, begins by simply wanting to do the right thing, to do right by everybody. His very selflessness and enthusiastic devotion to what he thinks is his duty leads him into his ever deepening imitation of divinity. The first of these demigods is a fraud; the second is godlike in his impiety; the third stumbles into a "pious imposture." But pious as his imposture may seem to be, it leads him into a Druidic ritual which in turn carries him toward incest, murder, and a hell in which he plays the role of the heaven-defying Greek Titan Enceladus.

After the three audacious would-be gods—Taji, Ahab, and Pierre—meet similar fates, whelmed by the elements, Melville creates quite a different kind of figure. Their bold and loudly articulate assaults on the Absolute are replaced by a meek, inarticulate, and mysterious being who often seems to embody the Absolute. The three principal incarnations of this being are Bartleby the Scrivener, the lamb-like man in *The Confidence-Man,* and Billy Budd. Each incarnation defines and redefines the meaning of god to man.

All the would-be gods of *Mardi, Moby-Dick,* and *Pierre,* the possible god of *Bartleby,* the apparent god of *Benito Cereno,* and the real gods of *The Confidence-Man* and *Billy Budd* have one thing in common: they are all, no matter whether they are modeled on Polynesian, Egyptian, Greek, Hindu, Buddhist, or Druidic myths, similar to and different from Christ. One of Melville's purposes in exploring other myths is always to evaluate the myth of Christ.

"Alma," the Christ of the religion of the heart, defines the central tensions of *Mardi;* Taji misses divine religion in his imitation of mythic divinity. Ahab takes the next step; wholly ignoring the Christian morality for which Starbuck speaks, he commits himself to the role of Christ's predecessor and possible prototype—Osiris, the Egyptian hunter of the demon. Pierre takes the final step; in his moral imitation of Christ he attains the crucifixion and apotheosis of a Christ. And in becoming Christ, he unwittingly destroys all whom he is trying to save. Don Alexandro Aranda follows Christ and induces Benito Cereno to have confidence. As a result, naked evil, defined metaphorically as the Catholic Church, makes of both Aranda and Cereno symbolic Christs to follow to destruction. The implication for Melville was clear: if man, in becoming Christ, becomes an unwitting destroyer, then perhaps Christ, in becoming man, becomes the Confidence Man.

In the first three major works, the characters create their gods: *Mardi* is a book almost entirely about mythmaking; the central struggle of *Moby-Dick* derives from a myth created by Ahab and the whalemen's imagination; Pierre, after his hereditary persuasions are destroyed, constructs from the pieces a god to imitate. But with *Bartleby* a figure appears who is perhaps a god, and *The Confidence-Man* depends for its central joke on the Confidence Man's being in fact a god. The joke is that the *Fidèle's* passengers are being fleeced by a real god, a god not only uncreated by them but totally unrecognized by them. Only the readers of *The Confidence-Man* know that a god prowls the *Fidèle's* decks; they alone recognize him, and they alone can define him.

Billy Budd returns to the central theme of mythmaking, but the mythic god created by Vere and his sailors is as much a god as the Confidence Man. *Billy Budd* shows step by step the creation of a myth, complete with the rituals and ethics of a particular primitive mythology. Melville's mythology has thus come full circle.

Man in the world of *Mardi* creates many gods and can be saved without any god. In *Moby-Dick,* man invents a god to attack, and this god utterly destroys him. In *Pierre,* the gods become meaningless, the conflict between the relativism of earth and the apparent absolutes of heaven becomes mortal, and man, in following what seems heavenly truth, finds none to strike, no salvation—only self-destruction. *Bartleby* and *Benito Cereno* pick up the possibilities of self-destruction, show how all forms of monasticism lead not only out of the world but also into the earth, and prove all the savior gods to be beyond man's creation. Thus sails the *Fidèle,* on which the Confidence Man, an uncreated god, enters the world to gull man with the earthly lie of heavenly truth.

But in *Billy Budd* man can again create his god. Man creates a god and then decrees, performs, and witnesses his ritual slaughter. The god is a man. His religion is a myth which saves man from himself.

From *The Wake of the Gods: Melville's Mythology* (Stanford, Calif.: Stanford Univ. Press, 1963), pp. 203-206.

W. H. AUDEN

Herman Melville
(*For Lincoln Kirstein*)

Towards the end he sailed into an extraordinary mildness,
And anchored in his home and reached his wife
And rode within the harbour of her hand,
And went across each morning to an office
As though his occupation were another island.

Goodness existed: that was the new knowledge.
His terror had to blow itself quite out
To let him see it; but it was the gale had blown him
Past the Cape Horn of sensible success
Which cries: 'This rock is Eden. Shipwreck here.'

But deafened him with thunder and confused with lightning:
—The maniac hero hunting like a jewel
The rare ambiguous monster that had maimed his sex,
Hatred for hatred ending in a scream,
The unexplained survivor breaking off the nightmare—
All that was intricate and false; the truth was simple.

Evil is unspectacular and always human,
And shares our bed and eats at our own table,
And we are introduced to Goodness every day,
Even in drawing-rooms among a crowd of faults;
He has a name like Billy and is almost perfect,
But wears a stammer like a decoration:
And every time they meet the same thing has to happen;
It is the Evil that is helpless like a lover
And has to pick a quarrel and succeeds,
And both are openly destroyed before our eyes.

For now he was awake and knew
No one is ever spared except in dreams;
But there was something else the nightmare had distorted—
Even the punishment was human and a form of love:

The howling storm had been his father's presence
And all the time he had been carried on his father's breast.
Who now had set him gently down and left him.
He stood upon the narrow balcony and listened:
And all the stars above him sang as in his childhood
'All, all is vanity,' but it was not the same;
For now the words descended like the calm of mountains—
—Nathaniel had been shy because his love was selfish—
Reborn, he cried in exultation and surrender
'The Godhead is broken like bread. We are the pieces.'

And sat down at his desk and wrote a story.

From *The Collected Poetry of W. H. Auden* (1945; rev. New York: Random
House, 1967), pp. 145-46.

Critical Essays

JOSEPH J. FIREBAUGH

Humorist as Rebel: The Melville of *Typee*

A SALTY, sailorly humor—a commonplace humor—a rather unsubtle humor—this is the first impression of the humor of *Typee*. But once we have said that it is commonplace and unsubtle, we feel how wrong we are. It is not the humor of a boy ten or twelve years old, making his first clumsy—and, to an adult, uncomfortable—essays in irony. And yet it is reminiscent of him. To that boy have been added a few years of adventure, a couple of long voyages, and, therefore, experience of forbearance and hardship and endurance—which experience, though it may have tempered the rebellious spirit, has in the process given it the double-edged blade of irony. Irony will be for the mature man a way of hacking through the over-luxuriant hollow reedy growth of life's event; for the time it is used with the clumsy uncritical lightheartedness of youth. Yet in both the irony and the manner of its use, certain depths, certain perceptions, force themselves upon our attention.

What do sailors most endure? And what, therefore, is the subject of their constant irony? Food. Food first of all. There it is, in supremely inferior quality, three times a day. On the captain's table, it may occasionally be a rooster fresh from the ship's chickencoop, though even then it will not be a very choice rooster. "His attenuated body will be laid out upon the captain's table next Sunday, and long before night will be buried, with all the usual ceremonies, beneath that worthy individual's vest." So nearly a corpse is this cock already, indeed, that a dinner of his flesh suggests only a funeral rite. But this spare cadaver is nothing, as food, to what the sailors endure.

> The owners, who officiate as caterers for the voyage, supply the larder with an abundance of dainties. Delicate morsels of beef and pork, cut on scientific principles from every part of the animal, and of all conceivable shapes and sizes, are carefully packed in salt, and stored away in barrels; affording a never-ending variety in their different degrees of toughness; and in the peculiarities of their saline properties. Choice old water too, decanted into stout six-barrel casks, and two pints of which is allowed every day to each soul on board; together with ample store of sea-bread, previously reduced to a state of petrifaction, with a view to preserve it either from decay or consumption in the ordinary mode, are likewise provided for the nourishment and gastronomic enjoyment of the crew.

About such ironical treatment of bad food, be it a scrawny rooster or miserable salt-beef, there is a certain mock-heroic irony—the incongruity of excessively elaborate language used to describe trivial objects of everyday vexation. The rooster is not eaten, but "buried, with all the usual ceremonies"; the "choice old water" is not poured, but "decanted into stout six-barrel casks." Polysyllabic humor is a young man's humor, for it requires sympathy—geniality—from its audience, and a certain freshness of linguistic response. Small children see the fun in long words. Unless in a convivial mood, adults often don't. Melville loves to use such words, both for their own sake and for their sheer incongruity. Sea-bread, "reduced to a state of petrifaction," provides for "nourishment and gastronomic enjoyment." Bad food always excites Melville to this ironic, polysyllabic, incongruity:

> . . . rummaging once more beneath his garment, he [Toby] produced a small handful of something so soft, pulpy, and discoloured, that for a few moments he was as much puzzled as myself to tell by what possible instrumentality such a villainous compound had become engendered in his bosom. I can only describe it as a hash of soaked bread and bits of tobacco, brought to a dough consistency by the united agency of perspiration and rain.

The "instrumentality" and "agency" of "perspiration and rain"—one ventures to suggest *precipitation*—have "engendered" more than a "villainous compound"; they combine to produce a young man's prose, a humor which only an excessive sober-sidedness will rob of its geniality.

If making a meal on a stringy rooster or a miserable hash of biscuit and tobacco excites such mock-heroics, what of that other awful taking of food, cannibalism? In dealing with it, Melville is often as genial as with biscuit or with fowl. Cannibals become "unnatural gourmands, taking it into their heads to make a convivial meal of a poor devil." Thus, before he has met the Typees; afterwards, although he is aware of "that fearful death which, under all these smiling appearances might yet menace," he is able to argue with Toby that "a more humane, gentlemanly, and amiable set of epicures do not probably exist in the Pacific." When confronted with the actual evidence of cannibalism, he abandons the humor of incongruity for sheer horror; but the horror has all along been implicit in the humor. . . .

Comparing and contrasting familiar with unfamiliar, a common trick of the travel books, Melville borrows for his purpose of humor by incongruity. Civilized words are applied to uncivilized situations. A medicine-man is alluded to as a "leech," that contemptuous colloquialism functioning as ironic commentary on quackery wherever found, in savagery or civilization. In describing Fayaway's becoming nudity, Melville evidently burlesques the prose of contemporary fashion-magazines:

> Fayaway—I must avow the fact—for the most part clung to the primitive and summer garb of Eden. But how becoming the costume! It showed

her fine figure to the best possible advantage; and nothing could have been better adapted to her peculiar style of beauty.

Melville ridicules not only the prose of the fashion plates, but also the fashions themselves. In describing Tom's costume in Typee, he writes:

A few folds of yellow tappa, tucked about my waist, descended to my feet in the style of a lady's petticoat, only I did not have recourse to those voluminous paddings in the rear with which our gentle dames are in the habit of augmenting the sublime rotundity of their figures.

"Sublime rotundity"—such deliberate bombast, such bland association of the ideal "sublime" with fleshly "rotundity," pushes satire by incongruity almost to its farthest extreme.

Incongruity supports Melville's primitivism; through it, he points out the advantages of savagery over civilization.

There you might have seen a throng of young females, not filled with envyings of each other's charms, nor displaying the ridiculous affectations of gentility, nor yet moving in whalebone corsets, like so many automatons, but free, inartificially happy, and unconstrained.

Women, however, are women, wherever they may be, and Melville is not one to make them over to fit his primitivistic notions. On an occasion of crisis in Typee Valley,

the women, who had congregated in the groves, set up the most violent clamours, as they invariably do here as elsewhere on every occasion of excitement and alarm, with a view to tranquillizing their own minds and disturbing other people.

Nor are women's foibles the only ones satirized:

as in all cases of hurry and confusion in every part of the world, a number of individuals kept hurrying to and fro with amazing vigour and perseverance, doing nothing themselves, and hindering others.

So Melville satirizes man: by placing civilized manners against a backdrop of primitive life to attain perspective by incongruity; and thus, by showing how certain human foibles are to be found in both civilized and primitive societies, he avoids the worst excesses of a Rousseauistic adulation of primitive man. . . .

Sexual arrangements in Typee Valley afforded Melville a fine opportunity for perspective by incongruity. He is more completely the primitivist, more fully the rebel, in dealing with these matters than in dealing with most other subjects. His humor on this subject depends again to some degree upon verbal management. When he felt the danger that his irony would evoke anger, he seems often to have fallen back on verbal tone to convey that irony. For, as he says, "Married women, to be sure!—I know better than to offend them." He writes:

> Previously to seeing the Dancing Widows I had little idea that there were any matrimonial relations subsisting in Typee, and I should as soon have thought of a Platonic affection being cultivated between the sexes, as of the solemn connection of man and wife.

In those two words—"solemn connection"—there is as fine an ironic commentary on marriage as one might produce. For it implies the sober introspective self-assured fulfillment of early matrimony, the placid interdependence of the matrimony of middle life, the indifference of later life, the permeating happiness/unhappiness of the state in all its phases, as well as the ritualistic, institutionalized gentility of the arrangement in its economic and social status. Melville's genius was able to find just the right pair of words in which to compress all that complex of meaning. Though in such matters there is no proof, our reading does his views no violence. The young rebel knew how simultaneously to reveal and conceal his rebellion. He has, as he says, "more than one reason to believe that tedious courtships are unknown in the valley of Typee," and the deletion of that ambiguous sentence from the American edition shows that his rebellion did not go unobserved. It was sometimes more direct, although it usually kept a becoming geniality:

> As nothing stands in the way of a separation, the matrimonial yoke sits easily and lightly, and a Typee wife lives on very pleasant and sociable terms with her husbands.

Perhaps the one institution more sacred to nineteenth-century America than matrimony was religion; and although Melville is if anything more outspoken in criticizing it directly, his humorous treatment of the fact that "the penalty of the Fall presses very lightly upon the valley of Typee" employs the same methods of rebellion. Kory-kory, the hero's guardian and valet, is his guide in matters religious and moral, comparable to some contemporary orator:

> Kory-kory seemed to experience so heartfelt a desire to infuse into our minds proper views ... that, assisted in his endeavours by the little knowledge of the language we had acquired, he actually made us comprehend a considerable part of what he said. To facilitate our correct apprehension of his meaning, he at first condensed his ideas into the smallest possible compass. . . .
> As he continued his harangue, however, Kory-kory, in emulation of our more polished orators, began to launch out rather diffusely into other branches of his subject, enlarging probably upon the moral reflections it suggested. . . .

If through Kory-kory, the oratory of the era is ridiculed, so is the rhetoric of the Bible paraphrased and burlesqued. Kory-kory speaks of a departed chief as "paddling his way to the realms of bliss and breadfruit"; and here we have another instance of Melville's characteristic humorous thrust—as decorous in phrase as a Gift Book of the decade, as entirely suitable for the eye of a young lady; and yet, in its mockery of the phrase "milk and honey," flippantly indicative of an underlying skepticism. The skepticism is more startlingly outspoken—although still phrased with ambiguous decorum—in the passage describing a sort of native Stonehenge:

> These structures bear every indication of a very high antiquity, and Kory-kory, who was my authority in all matters of scientific research, gave me to understand that they were coeval with the creation of the world; that the great gods themselves were the builders; and that they would endure until time shall be no more. Kory-kory's prompt explanation, and his attributing the work to a divine origin, at once convinced me that neither he nor the rest of his countrymen knew anything about them.

Mehevi, in explaining the taboo to Tom, employed "a variety of most extraordinary words, which, from their amazing length and sonorousness, I have every reason to believe were of a theological nature." When they did not excite his anger, as the missionaries so often did, matters theological excited Melville's risibilities. And his laughter, though mocking, had a quiet urbanity about it remarkable in so young a man.

> They are either too lazy or too sensible to worry themselves about abstract points of religious belief. While I was among them, they never held any synods or councils to settle the principles of their faith in an ill-favoured god, with a long bottle-nose, and fat shapeless arms crossed upon his breast; whilst others worshipped an image which, having no likeness either in heaven or on earth, could hardly be called an idol. As the islanders always maintained a discreet reserve with regard to my own peculiar views on religion, I thought it would be excessively ill-bred in me to pry into theirs.

Religious tolerance, seen as a quality of gentlemanliness, brings into ironic juxtaposition two conflicting aspects of nineteenth-century culture: religiosity and gentility. Anyone who really felt this tension must have been upset by this passage. Such humor could have appealed only to persons who had some urbanity as well as some of Melville's salty rebelliousness against convention. It would require the same sort of person to appreciate Melville's mockery of the self-righteous and horrified religious man's observation of a native's abusive treatment of a god:

> When one of the inferior order of natives could show such contempt for a venerable and decrepit God of the Groves, what the state of religion

must be among the people in general is easily to be imagined. In truth, I regard the Typees as a back-slidden generation. They are sunk in religious sloth, and require a spiritual revival. A long prosperity of bread-fruit and cocoanuts has rendered them remiss in the performance of their higher obligations. The wood-rot malady is spreading among the idols—the fruit upon their altars is becoming offensive—the temples themselves need re-thatching—the tattooed clergy are altogether too light-hearted and lazy—and their flocks are going astray.

Such burlesque sermonizing could perhaps have deceived some and angered others; but the heartier spirits of the age were probably delighted with the utterance of polished proprieties to conceal a probing skepticism.

Much of Melville's humor, which seems to involve little or no ambiguity, appears on close scrutiny to be something more than a lively anecdote to be enacted in the nursery, as in this account of native dramatizing and ritualizing of work:

> So seldom do they ever exert themselves, that when they do work they seem determined that so meritorious an action shall not escape the observation of those around. If, for example, they have occasion to remove a stone a little distance, which perhaps might be carried by two able-bodied men, a whole swarm gather about it, and, after a vast deal of palavering, lift it up among them, every one struggling to get hold of it, and bear it off yelling and panting as if accomplishing some mighty achievement.

The same kind of primitive response to work occurs in the charming incident of Narnoo and the coconuts. When Tom asks for the coconuts, still growing on the tree, Narnoo at first "feigns astonishment at the apparent absurdity of the request"; then "the strange emotions depicted on his countenance soften down into one of humorous resignation to my will." After considerable play-acting of this sort, constructing almost an entire mock-heroic drama of difficulty realized and conquered by the ingenuity of man, Narnoo easily scampers up the tree and gets the fruit. Melville tells the incident in the historical present—a fact which may indicate that he had related it often in the homes of his friends. Our delight in this story is based, fundamentally, on the antithesis of primitive and civilized cultures. Having made of work a grim necessity, to be shunned whenever possible—retire at fifty and enjoy life!—civilized man stands lost in joy and admiration of a people who make either a convivial game or a pantomime of a necessary job of work. This humor has something paternal and patronizing about it, as when a father's heart goes out to his children, whom he sees making a game of the activity which is his daily exigency. It is this tolerance, this humanity, which makes the humor of Melville's *Typee* so rare and so delectable.

"Truth," Melville points out, "loves to be centrally located." (And there he is up to his old trick of incongruity, in taking this phrase of real-estate agents and applying it to dialectic.) Melville knew full well that primitivism was no answer to the problems of civilized man. With becoming sailorly geniality he laughs at the primitive even while admiring it, as a father might lovingly ridicule his children's sober play. Even while laughing at it, moreover, he makes it the basis of serious reflections about his own adult and civilized sobriety. There is nothing startlingly new about making the primitive a basis for satire on civilization. A pervasive tolerant geniality however is the special contribution of Melville's humor. It suffuses his treatment both of savage custom and civilized foible. When he is genuinely angry, the humor sometimes becomes savagely ironic: the rebel in Melville sometimes conquers the humanist and the humorist. But in the main his richly tolerant humor is the palliative of his rebellion. Not that the two can be separated. A less humorous man would have been less of a rebel. Confidence takes its toll of geniality.

From "Humorist as Rebel: The Melville of *Typee*," *Nineteenth-Century Fiction,* 9 (Sept. 1954), 108-20.

HARRY LEVIN

On *Omoo*

TAHITI IS the principal scene of Melville's immediate sequel [to *Typee*], *Omoo:
A Narrative of Adventures in the South Seas*. Advancing in self-dramatization, the
narrator styles himself *omoo*, a rover; he resumes his interrupted tale after his
rescue from the Typees by a vessel designated the Julia and commanded by
Captain Guy—a pair of names which reecho from [Poe's] *The Narrative of
Arthur Gordon Pym*. Omoo, whose misadventures can be documented by
Melville's at this stage, joins a crew which is on the verge of mutiny, partic-
ipates in their protest, and shares their punishment: they are taken ashore in
irons and imprisoned. The island itself, so much exploited as a colonial outpost,
has become a corrupting limbo between two worlds, both of which shore their
cultural debris at the slatternly court of the barefoot queen. At the other
extreme, which is not far away, there is the Calabooza Beretanee, that most
disarming of prison camps; and Melville dwells upon its sorts and conditions
of damaged humanity as fondly as Dostoevsky upon the inmates of his Siberian
House of the Dead, or E. E. Cummings on some derelicts of the First World
War in his comparable *Enormous Room*. The polemic against Protestant mis-
sions goes on, with the bibulous Father Murphy upholding the decencies.
Shady Europeans, jailbirds and beachcombers, are concretely measured and
found wanting by native standards of beauty. "A dark complexion . . . in a man
is highly esteemed, as indicating strength of both body and soul." *Omoo,* for
circumstantial reasons, may make less of an impact than *Typee;* but it marks
an advance in control over more complicated materials; it presents the satiric
edge of the pastoral; it concerns itself with character rather than race, with
society rather than scenery.

From *The Power of Blackness* (New York: Knopf, 1958), pp. 173-74.

JAMES E. MILLER, JR.

The Many Masks of *Mardi*

WHEN WE first meet Taji, the protagonist of *Mardi,* he is a common seaman aboard the whaler *Arcturion* secretly choosing a comrade and making plans for deserting ship. He escapes with Jarl the Viking in one of the whaling boats—and so begins one of the strangest and longest adventures in all literature. After an interlude on an abandoned ship, which turns out to be in the "possession" of two South Sea Islanders, Samoa and Annatoo, a kind of comic Adam and Eve, the adventurers come upon a group of natives carrying on a raft a beautiful maiden named Yillah to a religious ceremony in which she is to be sacrificed. In the heat of his indignation, Taji slays the old priest standing guard over her tent and saves Yillah from the tribal slaying. There begin simultaneously Taji's deepest sense of sin ("guilt laid his red hand on my soul"[1]) and his highest feeling of bliss (Yillah was the "earthly semblance of that sweet vision, that haunted my earliest thoughts"). The bliss is not to last long, for one day Yillah disappears from the bower in Odo to which Taji has taken her on a kind of Garden of Eden honeymoon. But the guilt is to haunt Taji for the rest of his travels; and they are to be long, for Taji sets out on an endless search for Yillah.

As Taji's search progresses, the reader becomes aware that Mardi and its islands represent the world and its various faces and pretenses; and Taji's search for Yillah is man's yearning for a lost innocence, for a transcendent ideal, for the transfigured past, for absolute perfection, for total happiness, for a good unalloyed with evil—all unattainable in this world. Taji's search begins in Odo, where he lost Yillah but gained the king, Media (a fellow demigod), as a companion in his search. Three "ordinary" humans are selected to accompany the "demigods" as attendants: Braid-Beard the historian or chronicler; Babbalanja the philosopher and mystic; and Yoomy the minstrel or poet. It becomes clear when these three talkative if not garrulous individuals join the party that the search for Yillah is to proceed at a leisurely pace, as each nook and cranny of Mardi arouses their frequently prolonged comment, story, or poem.

The three canoes bearing this fantastic group make the grand tour of Mardi, touching all islands where the illusive Yillah may be found. But there are long stretches of the book when Yillah, except as a religious, political, or social ideal, is totally forgotten. Island follows island in a phantasmagorial, dreamlike sequence of several hundred pages, allegory sliding into satire, satire slipping into allegory. In *Mardi* the entire world wears a mask and things are never

---

1. All quotations from *Mardi* have been taken from *The Works of Herman Melville* (London, 1922), III and IV.

what they seem. The Yillah-seekers must constantly look behind the mask to discover things as they are.

I. Vivenza and the Mask of Freedom

The treatment of Vivenza, Melville's name for his own country, may serve as an example of the kind of satire (or unmasking) found throughout the long journey in *Mardi*. And, moreover, Melville's early concept of his own country is especially interesting as it relates to attitudes reflected in his later work. Before the weird caravan of philosophical canoeists reaches Vivenza her characteristics are defined in relation to Dominora's (England's). Vivenza is a "noble land," "promising as the morning." "Child-like, standing among the old robed kings and emperors of the Archipelago," Vivenza seems a "young Messiah, to whose discourse the bearded Rabbis bowed." But *seems* is not *is*. "So seemed Vivenza in its better aspect. Nevertheless, Vivenza was a braggadocio in Mardi. . . . For shame, Vivenza! whence thy undoubted valour? Did ye not bring it with ye from the bold old shores of Dominora, where there is a fulness of it left?" Melville closes his gentle scolding of his country—"Oh, Vivenza! know that true grandeur is too big for a boast."

As the travelers draw near the shores of Vivenza, they observe a huge inscription chiseled on an arch: "In this republican land all men are born free and equal." Upon closer scrutiny they discover a minute inscription in the nature of a postscript: "Except the tribe of Hamo." This striking example of the difference between appearance and reality in Vivenza sets the pace for the entire visit. . . .

II. Mardi's Maskless Man

As with Vivenza, so with isle after isle, country after country—the many masks of Mardi are examined before and behind, and always a disparity noted. Each pause in the journey precipitates a "philosophical" discussion in which the voyagers develop their views of the world, views sometimes subtly, sometimes violently in conflict, as distorted by varied perspectives. When the individuals accompanying Taji on his tour of Mardi are introduced, their distinct personalities suggest a variety of ways of looking at the world. Media is a "gallant gentleman and king," not only regal in bearing but handsome in appearance: "Strong was his arm to wield the club, or hurl the javelin; and potent, I ween, round a maiden's waist." Mohi, or Braid-Beard (so-called because of his long, gray beard), "was a venerable teller of stories and legends, one of the Keepers of the Chronicles of the kings of Mardi." Yoomy, or the Warbler, was a "youthful, long-haired, blue-eyed minstrel; all fits and starts; at times, absent of mind, and wan of cheek; but always very neat and pretty in his apparel." His dominant characteristic is his capriciousness, as he is "so swayed by contrary moods."

Although the king Media, the historian Braid-Beard, and the poet Yoomy become distinct, recognizable individuals, each limning the world with regal, historical, or poetic hues, it is Babbalanja the philosopher who emerges as the deepest diver and the book's one wholly unmasked man. He is described as a "man of mystical aspect, habited in a voluminous robe," and as one "learned in Mardian lore" and "much given to quotations from ancient and obsolete authorities." It is significant that he is introduced after Braid-Beard and before Yoomy: this "middle position" suggests the complex nature of the truth he ultimately achieves. Babbalanja is the best example in Melville of the terrible struggle entailed in the determination not to don a mask but to confront reality directly. To achieve the resulting insight requires a great deal more than mere passive acceptance; such insight necessitates an aggressive exploitation of all the intellectual resources at one's command. . . .

Babbalanja's insight into the universality of evil has an important bearing on the quest for Yillah. It emerges quite casually at times, as a major discovery at others. When his companions debate the character of one of the island kings ("There seemed something sinister, hollow, heartless, about Abrazza"), Babbalanja exclaims against the practice, explaining: "For we are all good and bad. Give me the heart that's huge as all Asia; and unless a man be a villain outright, account him one of the best tempered blades in the world." The lightness of this remark is balanced by the seriousness with which the same truth is frequently affirmed. It is this truth that is at the heart of the criticism of Vivenza . . . : "For evil is the chronic malady of the universe; and checked in one place, breaks forth in another." This knowledge is the one consistent truth Mardi divulges to the seekers. And gradually its relevance to the quest emerges: Taji's Yillah cannot be found wherever evil exists; and since evil is universal, a condition of existence, Yillah can never be discovered—indeed, does not exist. As Babbalanja finally tells Taji, "She is a phantom that but mocks thee."

The wisdom of Bardianna [Mardian sage of antiquity] is the wisdom of tradition, the accumulated wisdom of mankind; the wisdom of Azzageddi [the prophetic devil that Babbalanja periodically "possesses"] is the wisdom of the individual, of intuition. Bardianna represents understanding; Azzageddi represents "divine" insight. In maintaining a balance between these two means of knowledge, Babbalanja becomes Mardi's truly wise man, avoiding the pedantry of the historian Braid-Beard, the whimsicality of the poet Yoomy. In heeding both Bardianna and Azzageddi, Babbalanja avoids the mask of simplicity and acknowledges the complexity of truth. To glimpse the nature of reality requires both the wisdom of the past and the wisdom of the moment.

III. Serenia: Mardi's Maskless Society

When, at the end of the quest for Yillah, the seekers have reached Serenia, it is Babbalanja's vision, induced no doubt by his obsessed demon Azzageddi, that presents a true perspective on the meaning of existence on that unique island. Serenia is the true land of Alma (Christ) and contrasts vividly with the island which claims Alma, Maramma, where the voyagers discover a great gap between the claim and the reality: not only the Chief Divine but also the High Pontiff of Maramma displays to the world a mask of religious deception. After the visit to Maramma when Braid-Beard lectures on the history of Alma (he appeared "to the Mardians under the different titles of Brami, Manko, and Alma"), Babbalanja objects:

"For one, then, I wholly reject your Alma; not so much because of all
that is hard to be understood in his histories; as because of obvious and
undeniable things all round us; which, to me, seem at war with an
unreserved faith in his doctrines as promulgated here in Maramma.
Besides, everything in this isle strengthens my incredulity; I never was
so thorough a disbeliever as now."

Babbalanja's eventual acceptance of the Alma of Serenia takes on greater
significance in the light of his rejection of the Alma of Maramma.

As Maramma is Mardi's grossly masked, hypocritical "Holy Island," so
Serenia is Mardi's maskless society of Alma. In Serenia, the real ruler is "mystic
Love," and "true brotherhood" is the result. But the people of Serenia do not
cling to any false notion about the nature of man. As their spokesman asserts—
"But think not we believe in man's perfection. Yet, against all good, he is not
absolutely set. In his heart, there is a germ. *That* we seek to foster. To *that*
we cling; else, all were hopeless!"

As Serenia takes a candid view of man, so it makes no claims of perfection
for its society. When queried on Serenia's social state, the spokesman replies:

"It is imperfect; and long must so remain. But we make not the miserable
many support the happy few. Nor by annulling reason's laws, seek to
breed equality, by breeding anarchy. . . . The vicious we make dwell apart,
until reclaimed. And reclaimed they soon must be, since everything
invites. The sin of others rests not upon our heads: none we drive to
crime. Our laws are not of vengeance bred, but Love and Alma."

Throughout Serenia, emphasis is placed not upon an unattainable ideal but
upon a practically possible virtue. The society is characterized by its avoidance
of masquerade, by its cultivation of simplicity. "Pomp and power" are not
needed to "kindle worship." Faith flourishes without "priests and temples."

The conviction of religious faith in Serenia is exceeded only by its tolerance
of the views of others. Life in Serenia is not, like life in Typee valley, deprived
of intellectual content and lived solely on the level of instinct. There is
provision for philosophical disagreement. Babbalanja asks the fate of the
individual who disagrees: "But what, if widely he dissent from your belief in
Alma;—then, surely, ye must cast him forth?" The answer is immediate: "No,
no; we will remember, that if he dissent from us, we then equally dissent from
him; and men's faculties are Oro-given [God-given]. Nor will we say that he
is wrong, and we are right; for this we know not, absolutely." Life in Serenia
is not, then, a life of blind and shallow faith deprived of reason. When the
skeptical Babbalanja asserts, "Methinks, that in your faith must be much that
jars with reason," again the reply is without hesitation: "No, brother! Right
reason, and Alma, are the same; else Alma, not reason, would we reject. The
Master's great command is Love; and here do all things wise, and all things
good, unite. Love is all in all. . . . we hear loved Alma's pleading, prompting
voice, in every breeze, in every leaf; we see his earnest eye in every star and
flower." Man need not deny his mental faculties nor give up the life of the
mind to accept Serenia.

The reaction of the voyagers is immediate. "Poetry," cries Yoomy, "and poetry is truth." "Sure, all this is in the histories," exclaims Braid-Beard. "Thou movest me beyond my seeming," asserts King Media. Babbalanja, as he kneels, confesses, "Hope perches in my heart a dove;—a thousand rays illume;—all heaven's a sun. Gone, gone! are all distracting doubts. Love and Alma now prevail." Because of his "conversion" and his vow ("In things mysterious, to seek no more; but rest content, with knowing naught but Love"), Babbalanja is granted a mystic vision, the primary discovery of which is that "mysteries ever open into mysteries beyond." "No mind but Oro's can know all." Babbalanja is given the privilege of viewing Mardi's heaven, where man puts off "lowly temporal pinings, for angel and eternal aspirations." When he asks where those go who live "thoughtless lives of sin," he is told, "Sin is death." And when he asks, "Why create the germs that sin and suffer, but to perish?" he is answered: "That is the last mystery which underlieth all the rest." None but Oro may know this mystery. As the archangel returns Babbalanja to earth, he presents his final advice: "Loved one, love on! But know, that heaven hath no roof. To know all is to be all. Beatitude there is none. And your only Mardian happiness is but exemption from great woes—no more. Great love is sad; and heaven is love." Babbalanja's vision convinces him beyond doubt that what he had sought throughout Mardi he had found in Serenia. The truth overwhelms him: "within our hearts is all we seek."

IV. Taji and the Last, Last Crime

But Taji dwells not in the land of Alma, nor does he search there for Yillah. Is it because he has already glimpsed a truth he is unwilling to accept: that Yillah no longer exists? Such self-deception is nothing new in Taji. From the very beginning of his encounter with Yillah, he has manifested a fear of examining his own motives too closely. In his original resolution to free her, there is an unmistakable note of self-revulsion: "Need I add, how stirred was my soul toward this invisible victim; and how hotly I swore, that precious blood of hers should never smoke upon an altar. If we drowned for it, I was bent upon rescuing the captive. But as yet, no gentle signal of distress had been waved to us from the tent."After Taji kills the old priest bearing Yillah to a religious sacrifice, he glimpses but for a brief moment the possible complexity of his motives: "Remorse smote me hard; and like lightning I asked myself, whether the death-deed I had done was sprung of a virtuous motive, the rescuing a captive from thrall; or whether beneath that pretence, I had engaged in this fatal affray for some other, and selfish purpose; the companionship of a beautiful maid. But throttling the thought, I swore to be gay." And to throttle it Taji tries. But the thought recurs periodically in the horrible shape of Aleema's green corpse: "In fancy, I saw the stark body of the priest drifting by. Again that phantom obtruded; *again guilt laid his red hand on my soul.* But I laughed. Was not Yillah my own? by my arm rescued from ill? To do her a good, I had perilled myself. So down, down, Aleema." Taji repeatedly shakes off the red hand of guilt in an attempt to maintain his spotless soul. He deceives himself as to his motives and he deceives Yillah as to his origins: the bliss he achieves with Yillah is created from the substance of many deceptions.

In killing the priest Aleema and stealing Yillah Taji performs the ritualistic act of initiation into evil, the old act in new dress of Adam eating the apple. By the very nature of the act, the bliss cannot last, reality must finally impinge on consciousness, Yillah must disappear. To Taji, Yillah seems the "earthly semblance" of the "sweet vision" that haunted his "earliest thoughts." In their blissful haven in Odo, Taji wonders: "Did I commune with a spirit? Often I thought that Paradise had overtaken me on earth, and that Yillah was verily an angel." But there are intrusions in this Paradise. There is the haunting scene of the green corpse of the priest Aleema floating in the Sea; there arrives one day the mysterious figure of the "incognito" whose solitary eye fixes upon Yillah with a "sinister glance" and which seems to Taji "a spirit, forever prying" into his soul; and finally, there are the "three blackeyed damsels, deep brunettes" who come with their luring, sensual flower-messages from Queen Hautia. These intrusions press upon Taji a sense of guilt, a self-acknowledgment of the lure of the senses in his life with Yillah. Taji will deny all and maintain his innocence; because they are denied, these dark forces of the unconscious deprive Taji of his Yillah. In his refusal to admit complicity, in denying his own human nature, Taji deprives himself of Yillah. He cannot remain innocent and have Yillah. He sacrifices Yillah in pursuit of innocence and loses both.

Taji's flight from the three sons of Aleema, who with their fixed spears pursue him throughout Mardi, symbolizes his refusal to accept his human burden of wickedness. Taji's insistence on his own innocence results in the death of his two original comrades, Jarl and Samoa, who receive the spears meant for him. Thus the individual who will not accept his human guilt wreaks havoc on others. Taji's periodic view of the green corpse of Aleema symbolizes his occasional glimpse into his own contaminated soul. Taji conceals from himself as well as from the world the evil that is his. The visits from Hautia's messengers are symbolic of the deep lure of the life wholly dedicated to the senses. It was this lure that was hidden in Taji's motives to capture Yillah at the very beginning. It was this element which came to dominate their paradisiacal life at Odo. Yillah became Queen Hautia's because Taji's lust transformed her into one of her captives; Yillah disappeared because Taji refused all but a total innocence. Yillah is thus Taji's sacrifice to his own guilt.

Throughout *Mardi* Yillah symbolizes to Taji a total innocence, a good unalloyed with evil, an ideal perfection. And this Yillah cannot be found, not even in Serenia, because the human fate is involved in evil, human nature is steeped in an inevitable darkness. After Taji rejects Serenia, he sails for Queen Hautia's isle of Flozella: "in some mysterious way seemed Hautia and Yillah connected. But Yillah was all beauty, and innocence; my crown of felicity; my heaven below;—and Hautia, my whole heart abhorred. Yillah I sought; Hautia sought me. One openly beckoned me here; the other dimly allured me there." Taji has reduced the number of his choices to two, and each is an impossible extreme: he can never attain the perfection and innocence of the Yillah he seeks nor can he abandon himself to the totally materialistic life of the senses with

Hautia. In insisting on the perfect Yillah, he gains only the evil Hautia: in the very assertion of his spotless innocence lurks the evidence of his imperfection. When King Media exclaims, "Away! thy Yillah is behind thee, not before. Deep she dwells in blue Serenia's groves, which thou wouldst not search," he is pointing out the one place Taji rejected without exploring, the one island in Mardi where "love is all in all" and man lives reconciled to his own shortcomings and to the limits of his own knowledge. Such a reconciliation Taji rejects out of hand, as he ultimately rejects Hautia's tempting lures.

In the final pages of *Mardi,* Taji is transfigured from the seemingly innocent voyager into a monomaniac in mad pursuit of an impossible goal—but he maintains the pose of the sinless seeker. His mask is double, turned toward the world but turned inward too. Taji becomes a titanic fraud and his greatest victim is himself. He knows but refuses to accept the nature of man and the burden of existence. Man, less than perfect, is doomed to sin; evil exists; "Oro is past finding out, and mysteries ever open into mysteries." Instead of discovering the mystic Love of Serenia in himself, Taji observes his own heart grow "hard, like flint; and black, like night": "Hyenas filled me with their laughs; death-damps chilled my brow; I prayed not, but blasphemed." In continuing his search for Yillah, Taji maintains the outward appearance to both the world and himself of innocence yearning after unattainable good, but deep within he understands his genuine motives for the corrupt and fiendish impulses they are. Taji seeks to disown the heritage of guilt that is his as a man symbolized by his role as the slayer of the priest Aleema in the first encounter with Yillah; but in yearning to become all good, he becomes all evil, in attempting to be God, he becomes a devil.

In spite of Braid-Beard's warning that perdition lies ahead, and despite Yoomy's plea that he not commit "the last, last crime," Taji cries out, "I am my own soul's emperor; and my first act is abdication! Hail! realm of shades!" He darts wildly into the rushing tide and is last seen fleeing from Aleema's three sons: "And thus, pursuers and pursued flew on, over an endless sea." Taji's act is the supreme gesture of a fatal pride. In asserting rule over his own soul, he usurps the function of God. In abdicating his rule, he abandons his soul by deliberately continuing a suicidal quest. In shouting "Hail! realm of shades" he asserts a new allegiance to God's eternal enemy, Satan. Like Ahab and Pierre, Taji travels the path that leads from heaven's gate to hell, deceiving the world by self-righteous assertions of noble intent and half-deluding the self by an insistence on innocence. Like Ahab and Pierre, Taji lacks the courage to peer closely into the darkness of his own deep soul. In attempting to gain all, Taji loses all. In seeking total innocence, he discovers total corruption. In a ruthless quest of heaven, he wins his way to hell.

From "The Many Masks of *Mardi,*" *Journal of English and Germanic Philology,* 58 (July 1959), 400-13.

R. W. B. LEWIS

Adamic Experience in *Redburn*

IN *Redburn* (1849), the Adamic coloration of the ["jumping off" into] experience which most interested Melville became explicit. This has been remarked by Melville's best commentator, Newton Arvin, who observes that the boy-hero of the novel "sets out from his mother's house in a state of innocence like that before the fall"; and the voyage to Liverpool and back comprises for young Redburn "the initiation of innocence into evil." Here we are at the second stage of Ishmael's soliloquy [in *Moby-Dick*]: the exploration of the degree of sickness in the world, of hospitals and jails and graveyards, of deserts and griefs and "Virginia's Dismal Swamp." For Melville and Redburn the swamp is not a comforting assurance of nature's variety, as it was for Thoreau. Much of the physical and spiritual disease the young lad discovers is packed symbolically into the demonic figure of the sailor Jackson; and Jackson is introduced eating a bowl of mush that "looked for all the world like . . . the Dismal Swamp of Virginia." With the appearance of Jackson, the consciousness alive in the story passes from the opening mood of elementary cheerfulness to the injured tone at the novel's center.

But the emphasis in *Redburn* is perhaps less upon what happens to the boy himself than upon the wretchedness and depravity that are uncovered as existing independently of him in the world; Redburn emerges with, at most, a sort of jocular but puzzled ruefulness, like that of Major Molineux's disillusioned cousin in Hawthorne's story. The Liverpool through which Redburn wanders, growing ever more appalled at its stench of corruption, may well remind us of the plague- and crime-ridden Philadelphia of [Charles Brockden Brown's] *Arthur Mervyn;* but Redburn is more the passive spectator than the ludicrous reformer. What Redburn beholds in Launcelot's-Hey, along the dock walls, and in "the boode alleys" of Liverpool merely adds to the cluster of scabrous impressions that began with the deceitful pawnshop-keeper in New York and continued with the drunken sailor who jumps overboard on Redburn's first nightwatch and the plague which breaks out among the passengers. All these impressions become concentrated and intensified for Redburn, in the "foul lees and dregs of a man" which were all that remained of the dying Jackson. It is Jackson who reveals to Redburn the power of the scabrous, the terrible power of mental superiority when it possesses a nerve of the diabolic. "He was the weakest man, bodily, of the crew"; but he was the crew's bully. His power operated through and not in spite of his wasted appearance; and the strength of his fascination for Redburn (who is aware, though only very dimly indeed, that Jackson in turn is covertly fascinated by him) suggests something not yet articulated about disease in the world at large. Yet, while Jackson is a wicked man, as Redburn tells himself in his Sunday-school language; there is a still deeper possibility—that "his wickedness seemed to spring from his woe."

This conjunction of sickness and power and wickedness and sorrow is the substance of *Redburn:* these and the impression they make upon the lad's character. But if there is something more astir in the novel, it derives from another dead figure: Redburn's father—not from his presence but from the acknowledgment of his absence. In Liverpool, taking with him a guidebook which his father had used to explore that very city "years and years ago," Redburn sets forth to follow his father through the town, "performing a filial pilgrimage." The sense of his father becomes so vivid that Redburn feels that, if he hurries, he will "overtak[e] him around the Town Hall . . . at the head of Castle Street." Both the hope and the guidebook are cheats; the guidebook is half a century out of date, and his father is not just around that corner or any other: "He had gone whither no son's search could find him in this world." This is the moment when Melville's hero realizes that he is an orphan; but since the realization comes together with the discovery of the amount of destructive unhealthiness in the world and in human nature, it has little of the hopeful joy of a liberation from family and history. It partakes rather of the tragic feeling of the lost son, or even, perhaps, of the son betrayed.

We ought to locate the moment chronologically not in 1839, when young Herman Melville actually did visit Liverpool, but ten years later, when he was investing that visit with meaning in the writing of *Redburn.* For in that book, two perceptions which would be the making of Melville as an artist hovered on the verge of fusion—the betrayal by the father and the corruption in nature. These were the elements which decisively shaped Melville's treatment of the hopeful legend: what we may cautiously call the "objective"—the knot of hostility in the very structure of created things; and the "subjective"—the bubbling-up of whatever Melville had suffered during those dreadful weeks in 1831 when his bankrupt father went mad and died, leaving behind (abandoning, deserting, as it must have seemed to the bewildered child) a lost, helpless, poverty-stricken family. These were the elements and the perceptions which took the form of a growing resentment in Melville: something which only just begins to get into the writing of *Redburn,* but which had, as Auden puts it, to "blow itself quite out" in the books that followed.

From *The American Adam: Innocence, Tragedy and Tradition in the Nineteenth Century* (Chicago: Univ. of Chicago Press, 1955), pp. 136-38.

HOWARD P. VINCENT

White-Jacket: An Essay in Interpretation

IN 1849, Melville's renewed venture into symbolism in *White-Jacket* [1850] was timid—understandably so when we recall the censure heaped upon *Mardi.* But even before *White-Jacket,* amid the reportorial directness and hard realism of *Redburn,* we find a jacket described with emblematic significance in the opening lines . . . and later references in *Redburn* strengthen our suspicion that Melville had introduced the jacket into that novel for symbolical significance. Similar, but elaborated so that it becomes the central symbol of the book as well as the chief means of structural unity, is the white jacket of *White-Jacket.* The story begins and ends with the garment, which also appears reiteratively throughout the novel, a true recurrent theme. The opening description of the jacket is realistic enough, and probably autobiographical. Mr. [Charles] Anderson pointed out [in *Melville in the South Seas*] that Melville the sailor did not have to provide his own jacket since he might have had a blue pea-jacket at any time, merely by applying to the proper officer, but a letter from Melville to Dana confirms that a white jacket had actually been a possession of Melville's on board the *United States:* "You ask me about 'the jacket.' I answer it was a veritable garment—which I suppose is now somewhere at the bottom of the Charles river. I was a great fool, or I should have brought such a remarkable fabric (as it really was, to behold) home with me." Melville then was partially autobiographical in describing the jacket. This does not mean that he was not also symbolical. He says that it was a "veritable" jacket, an ambiguity which might include literal and emblematic meanings. And although the jacket was actual (veritable), not all of its adventures were necessarily actual. But they may have been symbolically real (veritable).

Whether or not in Melville's experience aboard the *United States* the color of the jacket influenced his purchase of it, we shall never know. We can, however, believe that Melville perceived the symbolisms of whiteness and employed them in *White-Jacket.* No one who has ever read the prose lyric on "The Whiteness of the Whale" in *Moby-Dick* (written immediately after the publication of *White-Jacket),* nor who recalls the blondness of Melville's heroines, Yillah especially, will have any doubt that Melville meant to signify something by the color of his jacket. White for Melville was ambiguous; it might stand for joy and innocence, it might stand for emptiness and terror. White ranges from funerals to weddings. *White-Jacket* begins with the white-innocence relationship but eventually grows into the white-terror relationship at the end, reaching that point through a series of grotesque scenes depicting rejection. In *Moby-Dick,* white is employed as a terror symbol from the first appearance of the great white whale himself.

But what does the jacket itself symbolize? Many things, it seems to me, but the first symbolism is suggested by the physical function of the jacket, which was needed by White Jacket (significantly, he has no other name than this in the book) as a protection against winter and rough weather. He wants to be protected from the storms which will inevitably arise as they round the Cape. Symbolically, he wants self-sufficiency, and in this sufficiency to remain aloof from—or above—his fellow sailors. . . . White Jacket's isolation, however, results not from any profound desire to know himself through contemplation but rather from his refusal to participate in the ordinary life of humanity. Though he achieves a momentary harmony, and a superficial one (since the most profound harmony is that realized through resolved dissonance), the evils of the *Neversink* more and more shatter his peace. What White Jacket was trying to hold and protect was the paradise now almost lost.

The jacket is also a symbol of pseudo-self-sufficiency. In a long description "Of the pockets that were in the jacket" Melville describes the garment in terms quite similar to his later description of the old Arrowhead chimney ("I and My Chimney"), symbol of the Self. For instance: "my jacket, like an old castle, was full of winding stairs, and mysterious closets, crypts, and cabinets; and like a confidential writing-desk, abounded in snug little out-of-the-way lairs and hiding places, for the storage of valuables." Every want seemed taken care of, so that its owner says, I "fairly hugged myself, and revelled in my jacket; till alas! a long rain put me out of conceit of it."

The garment fails him. High in the yard-arm, White Jacket almost loses his life when his mates below, mistaking him in his white garment for the ghost of the recently deceased Shenley, "hastily lowered the halyards in affright." To render himself less conspicuous, he tries to darken the jacket, but the captain of the paint-room will give him no paint. Another rejection follows when his fellows at the mess reject him because of his garment, "for, had it not been for my jacket, doubtless, I had yet been a member of my old mess." . . .

It seems to me that we have by now the inescapable implication that Melville was not only retelling the story of White Jacket's adventures on board the *United States,* but was also, consciously or unconsciously—it doesn't matter which—describing his own spiritual growth. . . . *White-Jacket* symbolized Melville's inner conflicts as truly and as subtly as *Mardi* and *Moby-Dick,* although not so fully nor so forcefully.

Herman Melville had, literally and figuratively, escaped in 1841 to the South Seas. This fugue is the substance of *Typee* and *Omoo. Mardi* pictures Taji's growth into life; it depicts the clash of innocence and simplicity with knowledge and complexity, a conflict which inevitably arose as Melville set the South Sea culture against western civilization. Melville had not found civilized realities entirely defensible. On the frigate *United States,* Herman Melville, Typee visitor, faced the world, the harsh contradictions of uncivilized civilization: conscious and deliberate brutality, hypocrisy of all shades, class distinctions and discriminations, and, although Victorian taste would not allow him more than to hint it, sexual perversion. This was a world in which evil was so prevalent that it assumed almost a separate identity. The *Neversink* (*United States*) itself stood for what was perhaps the greatest of all evils, War. "When White-Jacket speaks of the rover's life," he wrote bitterly, "he means not the life in a man-of-war, which, with its martial formalities and thousand vices, stabs to the heart the soul of all free-and-easy honourable rovers." Melville, his mind still filled with the idyllic innocence of Typee life, found that the world to which he was returning seemed a distressing contrast.

What made his return difficult for him to understand was that some force within himself had made him escape from Typee, had impelled him to return to this civilization. He had drunk the milk of paradise but he returned of his own volition to the bitter brew of the western world. Something within him had compelled this election, but he could cry out with Keats, and *White-Jacket* is the cry, "I hate the world: it batters too much the wings of my self-will."

The two sounds that range in his ear seem rather clear. The one, "a soft moaning, as of low waves upon the beach," carries the same symbolism as Eliot's, "I have heard the mermaids singing, each to each," or is reminiscent of Matthew Arnold's "Forsaken Mermaid." The other sound, "wild and heart-lessly jubilant, as of the sea in the height of a tempest," symbolizes the malevolent forces in life. The demonism is further suggested by the "fashion-less form" which brushes against White Jacket during that poised instant [when, after his climactic plunge from the yardarm, the brush of a "soiled fish" reawakens his will to live just as he becomes suspended at mid-depth in the sea]. . . .

"Quicker and quicker I mounted; till at last I bounded up like a buoy, and my whole head was bathed in the blessed air." Does not the fall from the yardarm with its succession of events (the bloody film, the passivity approaching death, the renewal of life) suggest both the great myth of the Fall of Man and the Christian doctrine of rebirth, "A man must lose his life to save it"? Until a man can take in all of experience, good and evil, he remains a child. Melville wrote his *Songs of Innocence* in *Typee* and *Omoo,* his *Songs of Experience* in *Moby-Dick. White-Jacket* clearly shows his world at last enlarged to include the lamb and the tiger. . . .

The fate of the jacket is important in clarifying the symbolism:

> I essayed to swim toward the ship; but instantly I was conscious of a feeling like being pinioned in a featherbed, and, moving my hands, felt my jacket puffed out above my tight girdle with water. I strove to tear it off; but it was looped together here and there, and the strings were not then to be sundered by hand. I whipped out my knife, that was tucked at my belt, and ripped my jacket straight up and down, as if I were ripping open myself. With a violent struggle I then burst out of it, and was free. Heavily soaked, it slowly sank before my eyes.

"And from my neck so free the albatross fell off, and sank like lead into the sea." Coleridge's lines describe an experience similar to that in *White-Jacket.* It is dramatically and symbolically appropriate that White Jacket's sailor companions assisted in the destruction of the jacket—and in saving him.

"See that white shark," cried a horrified voice from the taffrail; "he'll have that man down his hatchway! Quick! the grains! the *grains!*"
The next instant that barbed bunch of harpoons pierced through and through the unfortunate jacket, and swiftly sped down with it out of sight.

"To be efficacious," says Melville in *White-Jacket,* "virtue must come down to redeem our whole man-of-war world; to the end, mixing with its sailors and sinners as equals." White Jacket came down: one self was annihilated that a new self might be recreated. . . .

The last bit of evidence to support my thesis that *White-Jacket* is a symbolical account of spiritual growth of the individual, that it describes conversion to life, appears in the sermon, the concluding chapter of the book. As is well known, Melville's sermon chapters are generally compact statements of the central meaning of the novels in which they appear: *e.g.,* Father Mapple's sermon in *Moby-Dick,* "Chronometricals and Horologicals" in *Pierre,* and "A Book from the 'Ponderings of Old Bardianna,' " in *Mardi.* The chapter in *White-Jacket* is a brief essay on the mystery of life, in which Melville explicitly reinforces the implication of his finished narrative, that ultimately the meaning of life is to be found in the individual soul: "There are no mysteries out of ourselves. . . . On that point, the smallest cabin-boy is as wise as the captain." And towards the end of the exhortation, he clearly states the necessity for individual regeneration: The worst of our evils we blindly inflict upon ourselves; our officers cannot remove them, even if they would. From the last ills no being can save another; therein each man must be his own savior.

"Who," Melville asked Hawthorne, "has ever got to the meaning of this great allegory,—the world? Then we pygmies must be content to have our paper allegories but ill comprehended." Now the symbolism of *White-Jacket* may have been here ill comprehended, but if my argument holds, *White-Jacket* justifies a symbolical interpretation; it tells of the coming of the knowledge of good and evil and of the fall from innocence and from the unconscious grace of childhood. It is a study of disenchantment. *White-Jacket* is Melville's first sight of the waste which he boldly explored in *Moby-Dick* and *Pierre.*

From " 'White-Jacket': An Essay in Interpretation," *The New England Quarterly,* 22 (Sept. 1949), 304-15.

MILTON MILLHAUSER

The Form of *Moby-Dick*

I SHALL ask you to consider for a moment whether the answer [to the question of the book's having an inclusive form] may not be afforded by regarding *Moby-Dick* as a tragic poem: or, more precisely, as a deliberately loose and discursive adaptation of tragedy to modern conditions and a superficially prosaic form. I grant that this is not an easy definition to accept. What strikes the mind at once upon hearing it is a series of gross incongruities: the rough or grotesque characters, the humorous tone, the intrusive expository passages, the extreme length and rather rambling development even of the narrative portion; which are sufficient, one would imagine, to destroy any resemblance to Aristotelian tragedy, Sophoclean tragedy, whatever. Certainly there is a sufficient distance in quality, in texture, between the two! And yet this is no more than a surface difficulty, met by acknowledging that the classical model has been transposed (not always harmoniously) into a contemporary form; Melville himself forestalled the greater part of it when he adjured us not to wonder "if . . . to the meanest mariners, and renegades, and castaways, I shall hereafter ascribe high qualities, though dark; weave round them tragic graces; if even the most mournful, perchance the most abased among them shall at times lift himself to the exalted mounts." This at least suggests that he recognized a general disparity of vehicle and theme—recognized it, and discounted it. As for the medium, most critics—let Mumford speak for the rest—will agree that Melville's prose rises into poetry as naturally and as adequately as, say, much dramatic blank verse does; while the novel was simply the form—the outward dress—appropriate to a great narrative conception in the nineteenth century, just as the epic was in the heroic age. It may be a somewhat unexpected vehicle for the tragic spirit, but it is really neither an inhospitable nor, since Hardy, an unprecedented one.

And beneath this new surface, beneath the deliberately imposed Yankee twang, the *pattern* of tragedy is realized with a curious exactness. I speak here not merely of the temper, the tone and movement characteristic of tragedy, but of the formal classic definition. Sea-change or not, it is all there. Ahab, as ship's captain, is king in his own realm—Melville stresses the point—and his character, combining great gifts with a decisive moral flaw, is precisely that of the conventional tragic hero. The flaw itself, a pride that challenges the very nature of things, excites Melville's admiration as Promethean, but it is actually close to classic *hubris*; Melville recognizes that it is a flaw, akin to madness, and that it involves equally Ahab's imposing spiritual stature and his inexorable fate.

The action of the book, for all its wandering course, is, broadly considered, single; it stems from Ahab's character and leads to his destruction: leaving us, too, with the familiar sense that this destruction was at once pathetic, inevitable, and in the last accounting just. Pity and terror are aroused by the catastrophe; we see in Ahab both an individual and a representative or generic character, human nature tensed to its last desperate pitch, so that we are moved both for him and, distantly, ourselves. In the Aristotelian formula, catharsis is an end rather than an element and is thus hardly susceptible of demonstration, but it seems, from the manner of the final chapters, to have been intended by the author; and in my experience at least that intention has been powerfully realized.

Even in many minor respects, the classic form is paralleled or approximated. There are what amount to choric passages, for instance; the time of action is long, but we enter upon the story near its climax, and (once aboard the Pequod) drive directly toward it; the action of all but the early chapters is confined to the ship and the waters near it, and so presents, despite its wide ranging through two oceans, an effective unity of place. (At any rate, something of the effect of a unities-drama, the sense of an action tightly contained and pressing toward its conclusion, is attained, although through devices that are more nearly epic than dramatic.) The action, too, is viewed from without, through the eyes of a philosophically-inclined observer who maintains his distance: that is to say, dramatically; it is even worth remarking that he leads us to a scene of affirmation, of order supervening upon excess, at the very end. Finally, and I think very importantly, the sense of destiny pervades the book. The behavior of the whale is made to seem at once fated (in the old mystic sense) and determined by natural law; Ahab's will grips the crew, but cannot exorcise presentiments and qualms; an aura of doom clings about the Pequod almost from the first. Among the elements that most powerfully contribute to the characteristic impression of Greek tragedy is this sense of preordainment, of the implacable working out of what was written in the beginning, by which even the gods are bound; and this, by way of atmosphere and comment, is one of the most strongly marked and obviously intended traits of *Moby-Dick*. Thus, in a broad sense, the spirit as well as much of the actual letter of the canon is fulfilled. If we can accept the very considerable modifications of external form as, after all, minor—devices calculated to "reach" the reader trained in our conventions, instruments by which the tragic mood might, in a self-conscious century, be rescued from bookishness and artifice—we find a work that, in its pervading tone and general structure, realizes the essential nature of tragedy.

The advantage of this conception is that it drives toward the center of the book, admitting us to something like an exact comprehension of its special quality and power. The corresponding disadvantage is that, pressed no further, it leaves too much unsaid. The book implies a wide range of ideas, stems from a variety of impulses, to which the mere name of tragedy provides no adequate clue; it is a book that positively invites criticism on more than one "level." The interpretation of this work as tragedy will first prove helpful and significant if it can be made to accommodate these ranges and depths of meaning without sacrificing its own outline: if, that is, it clearly governs or perhaps even generates them, rather than merely establishing one more parallel and (so to speak) rival category to set beside the others. But this, of course, is also the criterion of its validity. The form of a work subsumes and orders all its elements; what leaves loose ends is not true form.

Now in general, if we except certain reflections of the author's psychological situation, these deeper meanings are conceived of by the critics as being either mythic, allegoric, or symbolic; and of the three terms, which I think point toward the same fact, "symbolic" comes closest to describing Melville's habit of imagination. It is not a question, as in *Pilgrim's Progress* or so often in the *Faerie Queene,* of the deliberate manufacture of characters out of similes; facts, for Melville, simply do have meanings that are not superficially apparent, and these meanings are not denotative, not susceptible of prose paraphrase, but poetic and suggestive. This is the vision of symbolism, which (unlike allegory) is fluid, elusive, haunting; which relies on unconscious sympathies and buried memories and atmospheric evocation; and of which myth is simply the extension (but hardly the extension by a single artist's deliberate act) to primitive and universal material. A beautiful woman may be, arbitrarily, Amor, Faith, or Victory, as the label or the tale directs; but the eagle and the serpent are symbolic, and carry their meanings in themselves. That his whale is such a symbol, Melville takes pains to establish; whatever Ishmael may make of it, the reader is brought into close sympathy with Ahab's metaphysical vision by the whole tenor of the book, and preeminently by the great chapter on "The Whiteness of the Whale." And indeed, such sympathy is necessary if the captain is to be anything but a crack-brained old man, criminally neglecting the duties of his post. But with it, he is himself a symbol, deep in tragic meanings: the brooding and ecstatic human spirit, defiant of all prudence and all omens, pursuing the brute image of evil across the enormous seas.

There is no difficulty in seeing Ahab as "standing for" that which is at once noble and self-doomed in man's nature, or the whale as "standing for" a hulking natural order which man perverts from innocence by his own fiery excess: none, that is, so long as we remember that these things are suggested, symbolized rather than metaphorically portrayed, so that the symbols move according to dramatic rather than representational necessity. (That is, the plot is not imposed upon the symbols, but grows out of them.) And neither does it violate our first conception of the story by imposing an independent allegorical structure upon the tragic one. *Moby-Dick,* if it is a tragedy at all, is a romantic tragedy: one, that is, in which the author sympathizes deeply with the protagonist, perhaps shares something of his nature, and, so to speak, sides with him. Such sympathy demands that the hero's character and conduct, though on the grand scale, be representatively human; as with *Prometheus Unbound* and *Hamlet,* the story will be particular but archetypal, reflecting the author's sense of our most profound experience; and suggestion and association, sprung from the central energies of our nature, will cluster naturally about it. So it is with *Moby-Dick.* Ahab's fault was to rebel against the limits of his nature, the conditions of his existence, so that he read his own passions into the lumbering unmetaphysical world, and there pursued them; this is the root of the tragic action, and equally of its symbolic overtones. The two grow naturally together, stem out of the same original conception. We must not oversimplify the actual creative process; it is scarcely possible to doubt that Melville recognized the symbolic potentialities of his protagonist, and to some extent deliberately exploited them. The lyric seriousness with which Ahab's musings are treated, the broad and passionate humanity of his soliloquies, the consciously Promethean quality with which he is invested: all these, not to consider such minor symbols as the compass and harpoon, enforce the point. But we need not suppose that this represents a separate intention, superimposed as a kind of afterthought upon the first. It is merely the first intention pursued to its depths. The symbolism is welcomed and insisted on, but it was native to the original conception, which is that of the destruction of a fated man. Ahab is stricken, lonely, proud, and doomed; he is the romantic vision of the noble wanderer, whose topmost greatness lies in his topmost grief; ultimately he is eternal—or at least Byronic—Man. But he is so not as a metaphorical contrivance, not as the lay-figure of a *Weltanschauung,* but because it was in such terms that Melville conceived of a fit hero for a tragic poem.

It would be misunderstanding the book, then, to turn to it for evidence of some precise, narrow, and coherent philosophy of the human estate. It is more nearly akin to Blake than Pope or Swift. Its essential quality is poetic; it offers us not a doctrine but a particular sense of life. Whatever lies beneath this reaches us only in broken hints and broad adumbrations, and if we trace it down it is less likely, the active principle of it, to be an intellectual system than a glimpse into those depths of creative intuition in which the ordered systems have their source. This agrees with the nature of symbolic expression . . . ; it operates largely through subconscious associations of which neither reader nor author need be too specifically aware. For this reason it agrees, too, with the rather indecisive account Melville's correspondence gives of the "allegorical" element in his work: an element, it seems, instances of which his friends could reveal to him where he had not suspected them. Like Sophocles or Shakespeare, Melville conceived first not of a thesis but of a situation, and then of a character to fit it: a situation and a character which bear the impress of his thought, but after the fashion of a symphony rather than a parable. This is no longer the self-conscious and transparent world of *Mardi;* here the idea lies implicit in the image, as the philosophy of the Prophetic Books lies implicit in "The Tiger"; and the image lives, following its own course, with a pulse and volition of its own. It would be futile to inquire the "meaning" of some particular episode, or even of Ahab's scar or stump—as though these things had been planned out in advance like a political cartoon. It is the great sweep of the action, the deep resonance of the rhetoric, that really carry Melville's intention. The anger of spirit against matter, a mind heroically bent upon an impossible affirmation, a titanic gesture and a titanic death: these are the "meanings" that, obedient to the demon within him, Melville was directly concerned to express. The form appropriate to them was poetic and dramatic; we are only conceding him that artistic competence which the power of his work so conclusively attests when we suppose that he cast it in perhaps the highest of poetic and dramatic forms.

What I have tried to establish may be summed up briefly. It comes to this: that *Moby-Dick* is, in point of form, a tragedy, though a tragedy drastically modified by adaptation to the vehicle of the prose novel. Thinking of it as a tragedy, then, should give us our clearest and simplest understanding of the book, and in particular relate its structure to its implications—the literal to the symbolic level—in a natural and intelligible way. It establishes the symbolism as subordinate to the dramatic design and yet inherent in it, rather than either primary or independent; and thereby it confirms the experience of that not altogether negligible individual, the sensitive lay reader, who responds to the book not as a tissue of philosophic suggestions but as a highly integrated imaginative experience. It leaves room, in so large a fabric, for later adaptations and progressive modifications of the original design; but it inclines us to regard these changes as outgrowths in particular directions of the original tragic conception rather than as intrusions upon and violations of it. And it leaves the chase, the story with its color and its drama, not an onion-skin of superficial meaning to be peeled away, but the very heart and source and center of whatever depths of meaning the book may possess. For the teacher such an interpretation has the very solid advantage of recognizing the book's complexity while yet providing a single avenue by which it can profitably be approached; but I should think its real recommendation would be that it comes close to representing Melville's literary intention and defining his accomplishment, and so permits us to see the whole structure of his masterpiece with a fair measure of clarity and truth.

From "The Form of *Moby-Dick*," *The Journal of Aesthetics and Art Criticism*, 13 (June 1955), 527-32.

CHARLES FEIDELSON, JR.

Symbolism in *Moby-Dick*

THE MOOD of Whitman's reckless address to his soul [in "Passage to India"] is the mood of Ahab, who also is willing to risk the ship in order to go where no other mariner dares. Ahab's voyage is an intellectual experiment like Whitman's "passage to more than India":

> Passage to you, your shores, ye aged fierce enigmas!
> Passage to you, to mastership of you, ye strangling problems!
> You, strew'd with the wrecks of skeletons, that, living, never reach'd you.

The difference is that Whitman does not really believe in the possibility of wreck. For him the "deep waters" are, after all, the "seas of God," and his "daring joy" is "safe." Besides, although Whitman talks a great deal about his freedom from all formulas, and although this freedom can lead to the destructiveness which he often likes to imagine, he largely takes it out in talk. His own associations of thought are actually not very subversive. He simply does not bring his antirational method to bear on really "fierce enigmas" or "strangling problems," and his results give him little occasion to question his own proceedings. Ahab, on the other hand, is involved in a genuine dilemma. While he is as much committed to the voyage as Whitman, he is fully aware, at the same time, that his defiance of reason can lead to strange perversions of outlook; and he knows that instead of passing through the "most solid seeming wall" of appearances, as Emerson happily prophesied, he may wreck the ship on the "solid white buttress" of Moby Dick's forehead. In Ahab the image of the voyager—the signature of transcendentalism—is at odds with itself. Ahab is the disappointed transcendentalist, knowing no other way of proceeding but shadowed by imminent failure. Whereas Whitman can proclaim that the poet's "passage to India" will unite a supposedly "separate Nature so unnatural" with the thoughts of man, Nature has apparently turned against Ahab, and he has no confidence that "the divine ship sails the divine sea." At the same time he cannot go back to the security of land. He persists in the voyage, but it is transformed into a desperate battle, which is only intensified by the haunting thought that his whole approach may be wrong.

Like Hawthorne and Whitman, Melville in his way is deeply concerned with this question of "approach." The first chapter of *Moby-Dick* is the statement of a point of view. Ishmael opens his narrative by identifying voyage with vision: the field of man's vision is the sea. Like the island city whose avenues all radiate "waterward" and whose shores are thronged with "crowds of water-gazers," the sensibility of the individual man opens onto the ocean. And the "thousands upon thousands of mortal men fixed in ocean reveries," who come from far inland, "north, east, south, and west," are united in their silent brooding upon the waters. Beneath the jocular tone these initial paragraphs create an effect of irrepressible need. The attraction of the mind to the sea is life itself as a quest for knowledge. "Why did the old Persians hold the sea holy? Why did the Greeks give it a separate deity, and own brother of Jove? Surely all this is not without meaning." The meaning is rendered more fully at the end of the chapter on "The Mast-Head," where another water-gazer, lulled into reverie "by the blending cadence of waves with thoughts,"

> at last . . . .loses his identity; takes the mystic ocean at his feet for the visible image of that deep, blue, bottomless soul, pervading mankind and nature; and every strange, half-seen, gliding, beautiful thing that eludes him; every dimly-discovered, uprising fin of some undiscernible form, seems to him the embodiment of those elusive thoughts that only people the soul by continually flitting through it.

Here the voyaging mind is fused with the world in a flux of wavelike forms; the identity of the self is lost in a pantheistic sea. Yet this attainment of sheer vision—in which, as Emerson described it, "I become a transparent eye-ball; I am nothing; I see all"—is suddenly dangerous. As your foot slips on the masthead, external things become alien, the empty spaces between man and nature spread to infinity, "and your identity comes back in horror." To submerge in the sea is to drown; the self and the world are two, not one. The voyage of Ishmael, though it lacks the desperation of Ahab's outlook, is crossed by a doubt similar to his. Water-gazing is a paradoxical activity—a search for absolute unity with the objects of thought, only to discover that immediate knowledge destroys the thinker. This is the "still deeper . . . meaning" of the story of Narcissus—to return to the first chapter. "Because he could not grasp the tormenting, mild image he saw in the fountain, [he] plunged into it and was drowned. But that same image, we ourselves see in all rivers and oceans. It is the image of the ungraspable phantom of life; and this is the key to it all." The image is not merely a self-reflection but the embodiment of thought, the matching phantom in the sea of forms. The phantom is ungraspable as long as we stand on the bank; and the ocean is annihilative once we dive into it.

Whatever hazards Ishmael may perceive in the alliance of "meditation and water," the impossibility of resolving the dilemma by simply returning to land is even more obvious in his case than in Ahab's. To send the visionary back home would be to invalidate the whole book. Ishmael is at once a character and the narrator of *Moby-Dick,* and he is a "voyager" in both respects. The concluding paragraphs of the first chapter are not only an explanation of the sailor's motives in going to sea but also a kind of rationale of the book itself as a "voyage." The narrator is immersed in a drama of which the Fates, in a manner of speaking, are the "stage managers," since he performs a part having nothing to do with his own "unbiassed free will and discriminating judgment." Will is the essence of self, and judgment is objective knowledge; but he is governed by the symbolic imagination, which moves in still another plane. Before him swims "the overwhelming idea of the great whale." In the sea, which is the field of his vision, the White Whale is the mightiest image, the summation of all the myriad shapes that succeed one another through infinite change:

> The great flood-gates of the wonder-world swung open, and in the wild conceits that swayed me to my purpose, two and two there floated into my inmost soul, endless processions of the whale, and, midmost of them all, one grand hooded phantom, like a snow hill in the air.

The "endless processions of the whale" are transitive forms that issue out of a fecund center; each procession comes "two and two," for each shape implies an opposite. To go whaling is to entertain these symbolic perspectives. It is significant that the narrator himself is flooded as he sets out to invade the sea. For, properly speaking, the moment of imagination is a state of becoming, and the visionary forms simultaneously are apprehended and realize themselves.

In "The Whiteness of the Whale" the ambiguity of whiteness—its mingled beauty and horror, as exemplified in countless ways—repeats the doubleness of the "endless processions," and "whiteness" becomes a synonym for fluid reality, like the "grand hooded phantom" of the earlier account. In this chapter Ishmael solicits the reader's understanding of his method; he must explain himself, he says, "else all these chapters might be naught." He is trying to define not only "what the White Whale . . . was to me" but also the kind of thinking which generates that ambiguous creature: "How is mortal man to account for it?" The apparent answer is that the double meaning of whiteness is a product of imaginative perception: "To analyze it would seem to be impossible. . . . In a matter like this, subtlety appeals to subtlety, and without imagination no man can follow another into these halls." He who would follow Ishmael must exert the symbolic imagination, for Ishmael's "pursuit" of the whale is the evolution of an image. Although the meanings that develop are disquieting, and the whole process tends to become a "fiery hunt," he has no other approach.

Ishmael, unlike most fictive narrators, is not merely a surrogate for an absentee author. Behind him, always present as a kind of *Doppelgänger,* stands Herman Melville. As Ishmael the narrator enters more deeply into his symbolic world, he increasingly becomes a presence, a visionary activity, rather than a man; we lose interest in him as an individual, and even Ishmael the sailor almost drops from the story. Ishmael the visionary is often indistinguishable from the mind of the author himself. It is Melville's own voice that utters the passage on the heroic stature of Ahab. This apparent violation of narrative standpoint is really a natural consequence of the symbolic method of *Moby-Dick.* The distinction between the author and his alter ego is submerged in their common function as the voyaging mind. In fact, the whole book, though cast

in the form of historical narrative, tends to the condition of drama, in the sense
that it is a presentation, like Ishmael's vision of the whale processions, in which
both Melville and Ishmael lose themselves. The frequent references to drama
and the actual use of dramatic form in a number of chapters reflect the visionary
status of the entire action. In the sequence of chapters (xxxvi-xl) from "The
Quarter-Deck" to "Midnight, Forecastle," there is no narrator, to all intents
and purposes; Ishmael has to re-establish his own identity at the beginning of
chapter xli. At the same time the drama does not take place *in vacuo*; the
symbolic nature of the action depends on its being perceived. This is the reason
why Ishmael is necessary in the book, despite the fact that he and Melville often
merge into one. Ishmael is the delegated vision of Melville: he can enact the
genesis of symbolic meaning, whereas Melville, speaking solely as an omnis-
cient author, could only impute an arbitrary significance. Unlike Hawthorne,
the Melville of *Moby-Dick* does not verge toward allegory, because he locates
his symbols in a unitary act of perception. Moreover, the symbolic vision of
Ishmael is repeated by the dramatis personae. From Father Mapple's interpretation of Jonah to Ahab's blasphemous rituals, the symbols take on meaning in
the course of perception. The pattern of "The Doubloon" is the scheme of the
book: under the overhanging consciousness of Ishmael, with Melville looking
over his shoulder, the several characters envisage the meaning of the coin. As
the various meanings multiply, we hear the chant of Pip: "I look, you look,
he looks; we look, ye look, they look."

Melville, first and last, assumes that "some certain significance lurks in all
things." There is no other justification for the survival of Ishmael at the end
of *Moby-Dick*. "The drama's done. Why then does anyone step forth?" Ishmael
survives as the voyaging mind, the capacity for vision, the potentiality of
symbolic perception. He floats on the ocean to which he is dedicated, just as
the entire narrative assumes the necessity of water-gazing. The white shroud
of the sea, the plenum of significance, remains an eternal challenge. Yet the
very fact that Ishmael and the sea are left as mere potentiality indicates the
deep distrust interwoven with Melville's faith. The translation of man and the
world into sheer process, which satisfies Emerson and Whitman, does not
content him. The doubloon is evidence of the reality of symbolic meaning; the
significance is *in* the world, and the significant world is generated by "looking."
But the meaning suffers a fragmentation as it comes into being, and Pip's
commentary is an assertion of real multiplicity. The diversity that Emerson and
Whitman easily accept as new "frontiers" of exploration presents itself to
Melville as a network of paradox. Traveling with Whitman down the open
road, "the earth expanding right hand and left hand," Melville notes that right
and left are opposites.

Not only does symbolism imply a complex of logical oppositions but it also
tends to obscure these real and important differences. While Melville hardly
contemplates, except as a lost hope, any return to the substance of the land,
he is uncomfortably aware of the irrationality of the fluid sea. The ultimate
horror of whiteness is "its indefiniteness," the merging of distinctions in the
insubstantial medium. For "whiteness is not so much a colour as the visible

absence of colour, and at the same time the concrete of all colours," so that a snowy landscape, though "full of meaning," is "a dumb blankness, . . . a colourless, all-colour of atheism from which we shrink." The totality of symbolic meaning is intensely present, but destroys individuality; its "atheism" is that of transcendentalists like Whitman, who, in order to become God-possessed, deny a personal God. By the same token, in order to unite themselves with nature, they also deny personal identity. Melville follows in evident dismay. Seen rationally, as an object, the world is inaccessible; but, seen as accessible, the world swallows up the visionary. Ishmael's presentiment of the danger of water-gazing is verified by the fate of the "Pequod," which disappears into the ambiguity and formlessness of the sea. Only by self-annihilation does the "Pequod" penetrate the whiteness, which closes above it in "a creamy pool." Ishmael, as though to epitomize Melville's position, almost follows, but does not. He is drifting toward the "vital centre" of the swirling vortex when the "coffin life-buoy" suddenly emerges. Ishmael's status remains provisional. He accepts ambiguity and indefiniteness—he is "buoyed up by that coffin"—and yet somehow manages to retain his own "identity."

If the inconclusive fate of Ishmael evinces a double attitude in Melville—an acceptance of "voyaging" and a fear of its full implications—the fate of Ahab results from a refusal to remain in suspense. Ahab's motives, which are dramatized as vengeance against nature and revolt from God, lie deeper than mere satanic pride. Beneath his ferocious mood is the "little lower layer" which he confides to Starbuck: he seeks a kind of value not to be measured by the arithmetical methods of accountants. Money, the medium of exchange, is for him a symbolic medium; and his repudiation of the "Nantucket market" is a rejection of rational thought, just as Melville's doubloon is opposed to the commerce of Boston. When Starbuck continues to protest this irrational "profit," Ahab counters with a still "lower layer." He draws a contrast between "visible objects" and the world in process—the "event," the "living act," the "undoubted deed." Ahab has taken quite seriously Emerson's dictum, "But man thyself, and all things unfix, dispart, and flee." The visible object is only a "pasteboard mask"; the wall should open, as Emerson says, "into the recesses of being"; the living act is fraught with meaning. And in one sense the death of Ahab is the necessary outcome of these premises. For him "the White Whale is that wall, shoved near." He does manage to penetrate, hurling his harpoon, and he disappears into the sea, "still chasing . . . though tied to" the whale. In another sense, indicated by the wreck of the "Pequod," Ahab dies because the object is impenetrable and his assumptions are wrong. As he remarks long before the final chase, "the dead, blind wall butts all inquiring heads at last." He simultaneously carries the voyage to an extreme, losing himself to gain reality, and is forced to accept the rational distinction between the human intellect and the world it explores. In either case he is faced with an "inscrutable" world: a mask whose meaning is enticing but destructive, or a wall without any human significance. "That inscrutable thing," he declares, "is chiefly what I hate." He hates both the ambiguity of the meanings that lure him on and the resistance of objects to the inquiring mind.

As the mood of the voyager alters, from love to hate, the world of the Emersonian journey changes from hospitality to malice, and the "living act" becomes an act of defiance.

All this does not imply, however, that Melville washes his hands of Ahab. If Ahab persists in the face of an obvious dilemma, and is thereby destroyed, the dilemma is the same as Melville's own, and Melville has not resolved it for himself. Melville can reprobate Ahab only as part of his self-reprobation, for Ahab's fury is the last stage of Melville's malaise. Actually, no final condemnation is possible. The largest paradox in *Moby-Dick,* prior to any moral judgment, is the necessity of voyaging and the equal necessity of failure. The voyage can accommodate the benevolence of Father Mapple; it is the "apotheosis" of Bulkington, the perfect transcendentalist, who is present as a "sleeping partner" throughout the book; but it issues in the satanism of Ahab, the wilfully destructive pursuit of a knowledge that dissolves into nothingness. Melville feels involved in what happens to Ahab. That is why he could write Hawthorne that Ahab's greatest blasphemy was "the book's motto (the secret one)": "Ego non baptizo te in nomine patris, sed in nomine diaboli!"

From *Symbolism and American Literature* (Chicago: Univ. of Chicago Press, 1953), pp. 27-35.

THORNTON Y. BOOTH

Moby Dick: Standing up to God

ONE OF the great problems for man since ever he first dared to think about it at all has been the basis of his allegiance to his gods, whatever they have been. Undoubtedly the most primitive, the most universal, and the most generally persuasive basis has been power. Even Jesus made this appeal: "Be not afraid of them that kill the body. . . . Fear him, which after he hath killed hath power to cast into hell; yea, I say unto you, Fear him." And after all, what appeal is there from omnipotence? . . .

Now obviously if omnipotence really exists, man can do nothing except what it permits him to do. By definition, omnipotence has the power to bring us to its will, smother all rebellion, even make us believe that its program is right when we might, if permitted to judge for ourselves, conclude on some basis that it was wrong. Nevertheless, the powers that do exist to this moment have permitted man to condemn and to rebel against, as well as to accept and acquiesce, in the program that they make available to him. And under such circumstances the man with strong moral sense, who believes he sees imperfections in the scheme of things, would seem obligated to speak his mind in open court before he is led away to the torture dungeons, if such there be. Two of the greatest of such statements, it seems to me, are found in two writings, one ancient, one comparatively modern, which have often been compared, but never adequately concerning their treatment of this question which is central to both of them. I refer to the Book of Job and to Herman Melville's *Moby Dick.*

In Job the universe is essentially a compact, tidy, well kept private estate of the Lord God: vast, yes, as would befit so excellent and grand a monarch; full of creations and powers sufficient to awe any man, yes; but finite, even essentially comprehensible and imaginable to man, and to God an intimate possession whose every corner and least laborer is well and personally known. There is no doubt in anyone's mind in the Book of Job that all that is, is in the hands of God; everything that is or that happens is his doing.

The friends of Job have a high concept of God: not only does he have all power, he also has absolute moral qualities, including an absolute sense of justice. For the problem of God's relation to evil, they have but one answer: since God is all good and all powerful, any evil must be the fault of someone else. To Job's friends, the only possible explanation for the fact that Job has experienced calamity is that he has through some private evil merited it. Any other possibility would touch on the honor or on the power of God, either an unthinkable premise.

Job's attitude toward God is formally most proper and correct. "The Lord gave, and the Lord hath taken away; blessed be the name of the Lord." "Though he slay me, yet will I trust in him." But Job insists that the easy explanation of his friends is simply not true. He has done nothing to deserve his calamities; they have come for some other reason. Job wouldn't presume to criticize the Lord. He wouldn't guess what the Lord's purpose might be in so afflicting him. The Lord God surely must have a purpose. Yes, the Lord is responsible for all things, Job's prosperity and his calamity alike, and for all that happens to all men. But there is nothing in my life, Job insists, which merits these present misfortunes. Job will justify his own ways, even before the Lord.

The pious friends are frantic. The young upstart who breaks into the argument with some slight differences in explanation is frantic. Job horrifies young and old in so asserting his independence.

In the end, nevertheless, Job along with the others is prostrate before the power of God. The only answer that they have vouchsafed to them is that God's ways are to man inscrutable, and against his sheer, overwhelming majesty and power, any question is presumptive. There are some suggestions that perhaps the universe is too big an undertaking for God to be concerned with every little event of human life: he must be managing too many other forces. This idea is not emphasized, however, and the suggestion makes little impression in the atmosphere set by the introduction and against the overwhelming fact that the idea is given in the voice of God—right at a time, in other words, when God is showing direct, personal concern for an individual human problem. The easy explanation of the introduction itself, moreover, is not offered by God as the reason for Job's sufferings. Job and his friends are never told anything of the agreement for Job's trial of loyalty. They are merely overwhelmed by God's arguments and power, the latter giving great emphasis to the former. The ultimate affirmation of the Book of Job is, really, then, that omnipotence cannot be challenged.

It is not this answer, nevertheless, that makes the book great. In going beyond this even by Job's time age-old respectable answer, the Book of Job provides a very daring statement concerning the ways of God to man. It dares affirm that there is no connection observable to man between material blessings and moral goodness. For the fundamentalist it offers the further possible explanation for evil: that God sometimes sends calamity to test one's faith. This is related to the perhaps more morally defensible one that out of trial may come development of the soul. But most important of the Book's ideas, at least as we are viewing it here, is Job's affirmation that whatever God has done or may do to him, Job will persist in what *he* believes to be right. "Though he slay me, yet will I trust in him: but I will maintain mine own ways before him." In this it seems to me is the greatness of Job: in this thought, and in the fact that God justifies Job in this stand, rather than the friends who have been insisting that to affirm Job's goodness in the face of God's hand obviously being against him, is to insult God. Only a courageous prophet or writer could dare proclaim such support from omnipotent God for individual exercise of conscience.

For centuries the private estate universe concept continued. With the Renaissance began a significant change. The universe within a short time became immeasurably vaster, infinite in fact—beyond the power of imagination to comprehend. Since Copernicus, man's conceptions of time and space have been straining unsuccessfully to stretch themselves over a largely uncharted infinite. Since that time, moreover, scientific methods of investigation have seemed to show more and more that most phenomena occur in immediate cause and effect sequences that can be formulated into what are called natural laws: it became ever less and less necessary to explain any natural event as being caused directly by devils, men, angels, or gods. By the eighteenth century, educated deistic Westerners had come almost a full 180 degrees from the primitive religions that put a god in or behind every object and event—each tree with its separate god to give it life, each lightning bolt thrown individually by some god—to the postulate that though it was God all right—a God in stature, though in interests or methods nothing like Job's—that had set the universe whirling according to law, he had stayed outside of things, not meddling, ever since. And of course for many, an additional step proved but a short one: they did away with the absentee god altogether and postulated a universe which had existed forever under its own laws.

The variations from that point on were very numerous, ranging from completely atheistic materialism to determined adherence to the most fundamental Christianity. But even those who still believed firmly in the God of Job were conscious as never before that there were other possibilities, and that not all men of intelligence agreed with them. Since the Renaissance, the Reformation, the rise of science, there has been no system on which all men agreed, no rock which every man found irremoveably placed, on which all could base their faith, as there had been for almost all Western men at least during much of the Middle Ages. And in the middle of the nineteenth century Herman Melville, examining God's universe in his day, found in the ocean the symbol of the near chaos which he felt that sensitive and thoughtful men were having to live in: fluid, shifting, largely uncharted, vast, full of dangers and terrors.

In this vast, uncontrollable ocean, each man has one small, green, gentle island full of peace, to which he can never return if once he pushes off. Yet, Melville declares, it is better to push off and perish than to so circumscribe one's existence as to try to remain on it forever.

Captain Ahab is one who has sailed upon this ocean, and he finally suffers great calamity from one of its terrible denizens. Like Job and his friends, Ahab believes that God is responsible for the calamity, and, profoundly hurt, he becomes convinced that God is malignant, deliberately hurting man. Then to Ahab comes the conviction that he is fated to destroy evil, or at least to strike back a blow for man against the evil powers that pursue him. He who would aspire to such an achievement must be hewn to huge dimensions if he is not to appear merely ridiculous, and huge and heroic Ahab is. Where Job has a heroic meekness and submission in the face of disaster, Ahab has a heroic personal pride. Job, insisting that he has no sins which would justify his troubles, nevertheless reveals not the least sense of deserving personal blessings, either. His lot as a creature is to accept what God hands out to him, though his misfortune may be great enough to make him wish that God had not given him life at all. Ahab is not concerned in the slightest with whether he is a good or evil man; the question just doesn't enter his mind. Ahab is hurt as men are hurt when a friend or parent whom they have counted on betrays them. Beyond the agony of his physical hurt, exquisite as that is, is the spiritual blow that can be inflicted only on a trusting man by a betrayal from those whom he trusts. Ahab is bewildered, personally affronted, heartbroken, one might say, that divinity should so mark him for misfortune, should pick him out of all mankind for such suffering. This Ahab cannot understand or accept. In heroic stature he demonstrates that resentment which any person who senses and values his own individuality is likely to feel at being wantonly bullied. The White Whale, the immediate author of Ahab's misfortunes, becomes to him the symbol of all evil, and he determines to destroy it.

In his implacable resentment Ahab reaches one point of heroism that to many modern men appears better than Job's response to essentially the same situation: Ahab will not be cowed by mere power, however great. Job lies prostrate before God in the whirlwind we have noted. He gives up any sense of deserving an answer from God concerning anything, and senses only his own inadequacy and presumption in having questioned at all. Ahab, interpreting a spectacular burning of St. Elmo's fire on the ship as a display of God's power, forbids the dropping of the rods which would divert the electricity into the sea, and instead seizes the mast chains that he may take the full charge within his own body. Owning the power of the Spirit, he yet defies it; redefies it as the charge builds to ever greater intensities; defies it even when he thinks that his hands and eyes may be burned away. Nothing, not even the direct and threatening manifestation of the power of God, can cow Ahab.

Ahab no doubt could have been created only by one who had a great deal of sympathy for such defiance, who had sounded deeply the problems that fronted Ahab, and who had felt within himself the desire to rebel against the trampling malignancies. But however much Melville may have expressed his own desires in the creation of the titanic rebel, Ahab's monomaniac defiance to the death is not the only nor the best answer given in *Moby Dick* to the question of how men can or should respond to the evil of the universe. Far away by the time of *Moby Dick,* far back in the history of man's thought is the private estate universe of God, well kept, familiarly known, completely ordered and controlled. The universe Ahab sails in is so vast, fluid, restless, that the gods themselves cannot control or even completely know it. Even Ahab senses this fact in his saner moments. Evils abound, not because God sends them, but because they are beyond the correction of any god, even. Man's sorrowful lot shows not the malignance of God, but simply the nature of things, of conditions which the gods themselves regret: "To trail the genealogies of these high mortal miseries, carries us at last among the sourceless primogenitures of the gods . . . the gods themselves are not for ever glad. The ineffaceable, sad birthmark in the brow of man, is but the stamp of sorrow in the signers."

In the total effect of the book, more important than Ahab's heroic defiance is such questioning of the absoluteness of the God depicted by the writer of Job—the God of whirlwind, lightning, the constellations and wild animals. And paradoxically, if God's control is the less, man's is relatively the greater. Job's God asks who has measured the earth or stretched a line on it; Captain Ahab has many reliable charts and sails at will over the ocean's surface, navigating with great accuracy. God asks Job if Leviathan can be drawn out with a hook; Ahab has successfully hunted whales all his life, has had his companions make a banquet of them, has stirred them up, has filled their skins with barbed irons and their heads with fish spears. And backing up these significant echoes mocking the power claimed by God in the Book of Job is the statement of Ahab that he senses a spirit beyond the spirit of power against which he is rebelling. In the defiance of the St. Elmo's fire Ahab acknowledges his relationship to the spirit of power, which he addresses as his sire. But he asserts also his dimly perceived, but definite, sense of something beyond mere power, something which will outlast it, something that also had a part in Ahab's creation, a mother who gives to him a sense of worth beyond the mechanical workings of mere power, and whose nature asserting itself in him causes his rebellion against mere destroying power. There is a god, he thus affirms, beyond the powers working directly in our immediate universe so filled with danger and misfortune, a god whose nature will persist when mere power has had its turn and has passed away. Thus to the problem of evil *Moby Dick* can give an answer that was impossible to the writer of Job: evil exists because the gods are not yet strong enough to overcome it; Noah's flood still covers two-thirds of the world; masterless it overruns and swallows every sort of thing it reaches, whether its own offspring or intruders such as the ships of men. "No mercy, no power but its own controls it." On the whole such an answer modern man is likely to find both more palatable and more according to the evidence than Job's. Evil, most of us think, is undeniably with us, and it often comes upon an individual far out of proportion to personal deserving, as far as we can tell from our point of view. Unfortunate "Acts of God" seem to come largely by the operation of natural law and by chance, rather than to be directed by personal visitations of divine "justice." If it is hard to give up the comforting idea that every good comes as a personal, well merited award from God, it is sometimes a gain in comfort to think that one's ills are not necessarily his exact deserts either. And certainly it seems easier to give up some ideas of any god's power, to see evils as coming because even a god can't prevent them, than to give up some goodness in anything divine, seeing evils as coming because a god wishes them to come or has no interest in preventing them.

We must respond wholeheartedly to Ahab in his sensing of something of more worth, something more deserving of worship than mere power. But in failing to rise above the misfortunes brought by the powers of the universe, in trying to turn his own slight power toward them in an attempt at personal revenge, Ahab shows himself unintelligent, yields himself in fact to what he recognizes is the less noble aspect of his own nature, and of the universe, and he is destroyed. If in Melville's oceanic universe divine power or desire to avert evil is the less, man's responsibility is the greater. If man's misfortune comes not because the highest god wills it, but because the universe is not under such moral control as can prevent misfortune, it behooves man when misfortune comes neither to accept and sit in ashes, nor to curse God and die. Ahab argues that for defiance the spirit of power can but kill, and that all are killed. But *Moby Dick* suggests and the experience of most men confirms, that in life there is something which makes worthwhile its continuance up to a point at least. Ahab throws away all the life he has left to him because of personal resentment to undeserved suffering. And his misfortunes really do not justify his mania. After successfully hunting whales for many years, he suffers the loss of his leg, a loss which embitters him and determines him on revenge; but even this loss, which cannot be considered overwhelming, comes as a matter of fact in a ridiculous retaliation during one unsuccessful attack on a whale. His boats splintered around him, Ahab in a rage attacks Moby Dick, the whale, with an ordinary knife having but a six-inch blade. Only then does he lose his leg. And had he had but a touch of Job's meekness, even this experience need not have been the end of him. Ahab shows now and again through his bitterness responses which hint that life needn't have been considered completely spoiled for him. He retains some of his humanities. The book also presents in explicit contrast the captain of the *Samuel Enderby,* another whaler, who has lost an arm to the White Whale as Ahab has lost a leg. He is quite content to go about his business, continuing sailing on the depths of life, yes, but not actively seeking out its worst evils. And as Starbuck the mate points out just before the final calamity, the White Whale even at the very last does not seek out Ahab; it is Ahab who seeks out the whale and insists on a final reckoning.

That evils must be experienced *Moby Dick* would seem to emphasize. Life is full of dangers and terrors like the whale, the overcoming of which is necessary for the lighting of all of life's glad times like weddings and parties, for providing homes and shelter and comforts: "Yes; all of these brave houses and flowery gardens came from the Atlantic, Pacific, and Indian oceans. One and all, they were harpooned and dragged up hither from the bottom of the sea." At any moment there may come, and does come for someone, a stove boat and a stove body. All life is an endless and intolerable series of whaling voyages, with little pause on gentle land between. And on all whaling voyages there will come times after the backbreaking chase, and the fearfulness of the attack, the intolerably long trying out of oil, the endless cleaning and swabbing, when the rest appears in sight—only to be spoiled by another call of "There she blows," which starts the process all over again.

But even in the worst experiences, as when one is surrounded by a whole school of whales, it is possible to find calm and delight. The innermost soul can bathe itself in a mildness of joy whatever woes surround it. It can sound depths, it can soar to heights, unknown to the coward who clings fast to the well charted land and risks not his soul on the unknown.

The independent thought of man can make him seriously question or deny outright that his Redeemer lives. But it can also free him from worshipping gods unworthy of him, or even from wasting himself in useless rebellion against them. At any time may come a stove body, but neither Jove nor any other god can stave while he lives the soul of the independent man.

Moby Dick thus offers one of the great treatments for our time of two significant problems: the question of the basis of ultimate morality, of whether there are standards which may be applied even to a god, to see whether he is worthy to be worshipped; and the question of how much man is, and how much God is, responsible for the evils that befall man. We respond with Ahab to the urge to strike out in some way, in any way, against the general cussedness of things. We respond to valiant old Ahab defying what we also at times feel certain are malicious agencies, defying "All that most maddens and torments; all that stirs up the lees of things; all truth with malice in it; all that cracks the sinews and cakes the brain; all the subtle demonisms of life and thought. . . . " We know that Ahab cannot win. We know that he cannot revenge himself on evil nor destroy it entirely for himself or any other man. But it moves us to see him try. And after the White Whale does drag him down, we can turn with new determination perhaps to our own less heroic but we hope more intelligent wrestlings with the individual terrors and evils of life, attempting to do man's part, which must be done if the battle is to be won at all, to learn what is the highest good, and to make it prevail.

From *"Moby Dick:* Standing up to God," *Nineteenth-Century Fiction,* 17 (June 1962), 33-43.

E. L. GRANT WATSON

Melville's *Pierre*

Pierre is a record (for a certain period) of Melville's mystical experience. It is the story of the coming of the knowledge of good and evil, of the fall from innocence and the paradisaical, unconscious spell of childhood; it is placed in a deliberately artificial setting, borrowed from the New England of 1850. It is more than the story of the fall, for with the fall from innocence of this modern Adam, comes a soul-shaking increase of consciousness, which could only come to one who has the legend of Christianity as his spiritual inheritance. . . .

Melville creates Pierre as the God-man, one who, imaginatively conscious of the tragedy of life, would offer himself as a sacrifice to right the wrongs which Life—the father-life from which he himself has sprung—has, in moods of truculent unheedingness, created. But there is much besides, and if the reader's intuition can penetrate beneath the surface value of the symbols, he will find, recreated in the substance of this story of the soul, the fine, ambiguous threads of the warp and woof of good and evil.

Melville, in this work, more directly than in any other, attempts to formulate what he has apprehended of the mystery of life; and what is particularly interesting and remarkable is that he has placed all his apprehendings within the scope of those symbols offered by the *domestic* human circle, thus indicating that the spiritual advancement of man still exists and has its origins within the bonds of the family. Or in other words the world-images created from within outward are all sexual objects. The elements of the soul are divided into the mother and her son, the father and the son, the brother and sister, and the young man and his betrothed. These are not simple in their relationship; the brother and sister have different mothers; the boy calls his mother, sister; and later, with the coming of the consciousness of the tragedy of life, takes his sister to be his wife. The situation becomes thereby immensely complicated, and to the end it remains so, and, as a true picture of life, unresolved.

[Parts II-V of the essay treat Pierre's innocent background dominated by his proud mother; his acquiescent betrothal to the pure and fair Lucy ("the pure, the conscious part of himself"); his new acquaintance with his dark, illegitimate sister Isabel ("the dark half of his soul"),. her symbolic guitar, and her psychological double, Delly Ulver; his disillusionment with the God-like image of his dead father; and his mother's growing hostility as he tries to help Isabel. Part V continues thus:]

Melville, in his elaborate thoroughness, devoted a good deal of time to the whys and wherefores and reasonings which bring Pierre to the final resolution of establishing Isabel, not as his sister, but as his wife. The directing motive is Pierre's profound recognition of Isabel as a soul-image; and it is always with the soul-image in human form that the lover wishes to unite. Although Pierre . . . has no thought of an incestuous relation, yet he would, to justify the deepest springs of his being, celebrate a spiritual marriage with Isabel. This is his desire, and his reasonings lead him to this end. With the awareness of things unsuspected, all values are changing, and though at first from habit he may adhere to the conventions of good and evil, yet these values, too, are no longer set and definite. It is not long before he says: "Look: a nothing is the substance, it casts one shadow one way, and another the other way; and these two shadows are cast from one nothing; these, so it seems to me, are Virtue and Vice."

Therefore, all reasonings apart, the fundamental cause of his proclaimed marriage with Isabel is his profound desire for such a marriage. On this point the whole story turns. To understand what follows, the reader must make himself as emancipated from conventional thought as is Melville himself. He must not believe that Good is preferable to Evil, or Sanity to Madness; but rather recognise that Evil and Madness may be necessary and indispensable to certain phases of development. He must know, not only with his mind but with his heart, that the "sick soul" is just as relevant to life as the "healthy-minded" soul, and that many sick souls are spiritually far in advance of happier, healthy-minded souls. He must know, moreover, that such souls as are depicted in *Pierre,* though they go (together with all their lesser associated personalities) down into madness and death, are necessary and valuable contributions to the life of Man. We can see that if Pierre had not married Isabel, but had kept his consciousness of tragedy and mystery as something separate (though loved and recognised) from his directing soul, then madness and misery would not have inevitably followed, but we can not say it would have been *better* thus. Melville has given us the privilege of seeing another kind of happening, one which is rich in a transcendent beauty. . . .

At this critical period, Pierre must break, if need be, with all ties and affections of the past; he will proclaim Isabel as his wife, and accept the ordeal which will prove for him the transvaluation of all values: he is thus impelled by the facts of his experience. It is suggested that because fictitiously he had tried to put his mother in the domestic relation of a sister, so now he would make his sister into a wife. This is interesting to consider in its symbolic value. He does not know fully, though he apprehends vaguely the tragedies which lie in his path. He is impelled by the innermost forces in himself; and as the guitar answers to the voice and presence of Isabel, so he hears the deep voice of her being calling him from "the immense distances of the air, and there seemed no veto of the earth that could forbid her heavenly claim." Hers is "the unmistakable, unsuppressable cry of the Godhead speaking through his soul." And while he answers this call, his conscious self would guard the memory of his father. Thereby it is suggested that he would keep justified his vision of life, while realising that the acts and nature of life should be kept secret.

To Lucy he first makes known his changed condition. His words are short, merely announcing that he is married. He speaks, knowing that he must blast her and at this moment his earlier consciousness of a happy and innocent world falls, as does Lucy, into a swoon; she seems almost utterly to be destroyed. The vision of innocence fades before the rivalry of experience, and he is impelled to risk the death of part of his own soul.

He goes directly to his mother's mansion; in the same short words he tells her he is married. Mrs. Glendinning's pride and haughtiness rise to the rebuke. "My dark soul," she says, "prophesied something dark. If already thou hast not found other lodgement, and other table than this house supplies, then seek it straight. Beneath my roof and at my table, he who was once Pierre Glendinning no more puts himself." For Mrs. Glendinning, Pierre's wife, whoever she be, whom he has taken without her (Mrs. Glendinning's) consent, is a dark, *unknown thing,* as indeed the Spirit of Tragedy awake within an individual soul is dark and unknown to herd-consciousness.

VI

Disinherited by his mother, he returns to Isabel, assuring her that all loss for her sake is gain, for "she is of that fine, unshared stuff of which God makes his seraphim." He goes together with her and Delly to the village inn. Delly he has also taken under his protection, for he perceives that she is indubitably associated with Isabel, and must from now on be her handmaiden. To the inn he brought all his private papers together with the betraying portrait of his father. These he now burns, that he may have no unnecessary weight from the past to burden his soul. This accomplished, he prepares for the journey to the city. Very early the next morning they enter the stage coach, and travel throughout the day. During this fateful journey they are all silent. Delly and Isabel sit with faces averted, and Pierre, plunged in gloomy contemplation of the bivalent nature of life, broods over the evils he has been forced to visit on Lucy and his mother in following what so clearly seems his best and most commanding impulse. In this mood of despondency his fingers close on a pamphlet, or rather on a fragment of a pamphlet, left by some former traveller. He looks at it at first unseeingly, but after a while begins to read with increasing interest.

This pamphlet is a lecture by one Plotinus Plinlimmon. It is the first of three hundred and thirty-three lectures and is entitled: *Chronometricals and Horologicals. . . .*

The writer contrasts those values which condition and rule in the universe of transcendental Being with those others, which in the practical way of life, are found convenient in the every-day world of Becoming; and he suggests that since we are willy nilly in the world of Becoming, we can not in practice live by the transcendental values of that greater universe which our souls apprehend, without doing evil to both ourselves and others.

Pierre reads and understands more than he is aware of at the time; indeed he carries the understanding of that pamphlet in his unconscious to determine his later acts. It is this that sets him a little bit aslant from his line of transcendental idealism, makes him a rebel against the destiny which is the guerdon of an enlarged and religious consciousness, inculcating a doctrine of exalted and aloof non-benevolence. Thus Pierre, under the influence of a philosophy which is not his by nature to fulfil, fails, both in the world of ordinary human values, and in that other universe of all-accepting, Christ-like love to which he has aspired. There are hints here, developed more fully in the following story, which throw interesting illuminings on Melville's psychology. He is a deep searcher into the ways of life, the purity of whose perception is in some way clouded. Men such as Meister Eckhart and Jacob Behmen, are mystics both by nature and circumstance. Melville seems rather to be primarily a thinker, who by the accident of deep experience has become a mystic. He is never quite content to be led solely by the inner light, and though he is enough of a mystic to know that he can not rely upon the conclusions of thought, there are always not far distant, even in his most mystic moods, conscious strivings which sometimes seem to further his search and sometimes to drive him the more recklessly into a region of oblivion. Of this region he writes:

> But the example of many minds, forever lost, like undiscoverable Arctic explorers, amid those treacherous regions, warns us entirely away from them; and we learn that it is not for man to follow the trail of Truth too far, since by so doing he entirely loses the directing compass of his mind; for arrived at the Pole, to whose barrenness only it points, there, the needle indifferently respects all points of the horizon alike.

This is not the mystic speaking but the baffled thinker, and it is the thinker in Pierre who understands the pamphlet of Plotinus Plinlimmon. This thinker is at variance with the mystic acceptance of either Isabel or Lucy. He does not accept the child-like and twice-born wisdom of either his dark or his bright angel; he *thinks,* continually he thinks, and will not rest from thinking; his thought would persuade him to the attitude of a man who would master space and time with an aloof non-benevolence; his mind persuades him of the possibility of such a mastery, and at critical moments he hesitates between the polite, non-benevolent and aloof masterliness of Plinlimmon, and the tragic acceptance of the *Untergang* that the embracing of the religious principle involves. This is the tragedy of a divided nature, and Melville, in writing *Pierre,* has set down a large portion of his own psychic history. In the end of this story, though neither triumphant nor serene but passionately grasping at despair and self-immolation, poor Pierre declares himself neuter; the twin angels of his soul have both of them fallen into decline.

VII

But many things happen before the end, and the complex events which follow are often not obvious of interpretation; yet the inner reality is always to be found, and, once found, is far more significant than the surface happen-

ings of the story. These latter often seem wild and fantastic, crowded with
continual use of symbolism; often the smallest details shine with significance.
New characters are introduced; representing tendencies or complexes within
the *psyche*. Isolated and individualised, they stand out the clearer, and can be
the more easily grouped to show the intense inner conflict.

Glen Stanley is the respectable counterpart and worldly double of Pierre, just
as Delly is the sensual double of Isabel. These seemingly separate personalities
only amplify one human consciousness. . . .

[Part VII continues with the symbolic difficulties of the characters in the
city, while Part VIII deals with the arrival there of Lucy (Pierre's "innocent
consciousness" as opposed to Isabel, his "seductive . . . unconscious") and then
proceeds thus:]

Pierre continues to work on at his book. In this work, in his cold, isolated
room, he is cut off from both Lucy and Isabel; their offered helps he refuses.
Lucy, now occupying the empty room on the other side of the kitchen, works
at a secret portrait. Isabel gives an involuntary homage to the heavenly virtue
of her rival; even her guitar answers sometimes when Lucy speaks; and Delly,
the almost mute, unconscious vital-dynamism of this strange trio, cooks for and
waits upon them all.

The stage is set for the last and fatal struggle of these inner forces, and it
were well to review our former analysis and carry it further. Pierre's mother
is the world-substance which enfolds him: under her sway he is still in the
womb. He must free himself, and with the coming of a larger, individual
consciousness, burst the husk. In that act lies the cause of his mother's death.
He would seem to discover an outlet for growth in Isabel, and with growth,
freedom. She is for him, in that first contact, the consciousness of the tragic
aspect of life, and also the channel of contact with all the mysteriousness of
unknown forces. But she is more than this, and, if we look closely, we shall
see an interesting relation between Pierre's mother and Isabel. Isabel is, as it
were, the complement, and not the opposite of his mother, and, as the complement, is of the same material. The incestuous relation is still retained, and in
place of a mother Pierre has substituted a sister; his introversion in relation
to the sister, and his espousing her as his wife, is a disguised incest-tendency
towards his mother. Not only have we the incest-tendency shown clearly, but
the incest-prohibition, for he renounces both Isabel and Lucy and with them
the complete erotic experience, in order that he may remain a child. The
mother-material which is in Isabel, namely the mysteriousness, the beauty, and
the divine-seeming moods of indolence are of *danger* to Pierre. At the last, with
the vial of poison in her bosom, she names herself, the murderer of Pierre.

But all this, it must be clearly understood, has no part in actuality. This is
not intended as a simple story of the freeing from the physical mother, as
perhaps some schools of psycho-analysts would name it. It is the story of a
conscious soul attempting to draw itself free from the psychic world-material
in which most of mankind is unconsciously always wrapped and enfolded, as
a foetus in the womb. Melville would draw the history and the tragedy of a

soul seeking freedom outside (or rather apart from) the world-substance. And here we find an analogy in the book which immediately precedes *Pierre*. In this comparison we see that, as the mysterious Isabel is a danger and a final destruction to the virtuous Pierre (Pierre, who is Melville's representation of the God-man), so the mysterious white whale in *Moby Dick* is a danger and an ultimate destruction to Ahab and all his crew (Ahab being the Man-god). Isabel is of the same world-substance (mother-substance) as Moby Dick; the aspect from which they are viewed constituting the difference. Their mystery, their attractiveness and their all-engulfing destructiveness is the same. If we have understood the books aright, we see them as complementary aspects of the same problem. And here again it should be emphasised that Isabel is no more a symbol of *evil* than is the white whale. In both these books Melville is dealing with life-values which are beyond good and evil. Only from the terrestrially human standpoint, and still enwrapped in that same mother-substance of the world, do these words have any meaning.

Lucy, with her heavenly love and her heavenly acceptance of the event, is an essence direct from the universe of transcendental Being; and although, as Pierre's innocence of conscience, she was framed to save him from the brother-sister incest relation, which, as we have seen, is reversion into the world-substance, she is of too heavenly a nature to offer adequate compensation to the lure of Isabel. She is too pure and too frail in her earthly manifestation. In actuality she has not earthly strength enough to portray him as he should be *in the flesh;* she draws him only in the skeleton. And, when at the crisis of his fate he bursts in to see the portrait, she sits mute and unmoving, allowing him to rush away *from her* to his destruction.

Attended upon each hand by these familiars (his heavenly and his earthly Aphrodite) Pierre still works at his book, seeking to find in thought a deliverance from his fate, his fate sealed already by his union with Isabel. His forces fail him; he can do no more. "A general and nameless torpor seems stealing upon him."

In this state of semi-consciousness he has a vision, in which are contrasted man's earthly household, peace and the ever-encroaching appetite of God; here is given (symbol of Pierre as a thinker) the giant Enceladus, who would storm the heavenly heights, and regain his paternal birthright even by fierce escalade, but who is overthrown by the gods themselves, with a mountain heaved upon his back, and pinned to the earth. As Enceladus he sees himself battering the steeps of heaven with his bare, armless torso. . . .

From this vision Pierre rises and, on an impulse, offers to take his two companions out into the city. Isabel is overjoyed that he has left his "hateful book." She hates it as part of the realm of thought, and thus opposed to her. Pierre offers to take them out on the sea—a desire for further contact with the unconscious. This last passage is so tremendously charged with events and symbolic significance that it should be read carefully and in detail. Every detail counts, and not only what is written, but the great silent vistas between the words, these need all faculties to grasp their suggestiveness. The mysterious picture of a *foreigner,* that to Pierre resembles the portrait of his father, and to Isabel resembles her memory of her father, when he came to see her at the farm after she had left the asylum, this foreign picture clothes the image of the father in yet further ambiguousness; and this is further enhanced by Lucy's preoccupation with the copy of Guido's "Beatrice Cenci." These two pictures front one another on opposite sides of the gallery, "so that in secret they seemed to be pantomimically talking over the heads of the living spectators below." This, in the light of recent psychological research, is significant enough, and significant, too, Isabel's excitement at the motion of the boat, and her desire to plunge over the side and float away into the blue profound where sky and sea meet.

The end comes swiftly. Pierre, who has been wrought to the uttermost extreme of exasperation by the hostile gestures of his double, Glen Stanley, now ruthlessly murders that part of himself which Glen symbolises, and in so doing: "His own hand had extinguished his house in slaughtering the only unoutlawed human being by the name of Glendinning." After this action of inner violence he falls into a self-shut-in state of gloom and despondency, well symbolised by the prison. But even in prison he is attended by his two angels; Lucy, so long as sanity remains, will ever cleave to his soul, however great his despair, and Isabel is that deeper part which can not be separated even by death or madness. Enveloped by the uttermost despair, and surrounded by the ruin which has become his fate, he knows them, in a light of a newly-won wisdom, as the Fool of Virtue and the Fool of Truth. Himself, as the Fool of Fate, has already repudiated them both.

From "Melville's *Pierre,*" *The New England Quarterly,* 3 (April 1930), 195-234.

ROBERT M. FARNSWORTH

Israel Potter: Pathetic Comedy

Israel Potter is a very uneven book, but it is a serious projection of Melville's beliefs and assumptions in that ambiguous, but fascinating, phase of his career which followed *Pierre* and which shows him emerging as a master of irony.

Matthiessen [*The American Renaissance* 491] may be right when he suggests that *Israel Potter* was written "under a miserable compulsion"; but if so it is certainly the same compulsion which caused Melville to write *Pierre* as well as *Israel Potter* and *The Confidence Man,* and contrary to Matthiessen's indication Melville gained increasing control over the compulsion and so was increasingly able to write the kind of books he wanted to. *Pierre,* despite its terrible power, is a failure because Melville's irony is not effectively controlled. Melville intended in *Pierre* to surpass the cosmic significance of *Moby-Dick,* but he did not have the technical tools to accomplish his goal. As a consequence *Pierre* is often grotesque and painful. Melville is thrown while wrestling with his angel, Art. In *Israel Potter* Melville selects an opponent more his size to try new holds and measure their effect. The rage, anguish, and nausea of *Pierre* are too intensely an essential part of Melville's feeling toward his world at this time of his life to be abandoned or radically changed, but in *Israel Potter* he brings them under greater control by focussing them ironically in the soft light of pathetic comedy.

Just prior to his description of the engagement between the *Serapis* and the *Bon Homme Richard,* in many respects the climactic scene of the novel, Melville says of John Paul Jones:

> The career of this stubborn adventurer signally illustrates the idea that since all human affairs are subject to organic disorder, since they are created in and sustained by a sort of half-disciplined chaos, hence he who in great things seeks success must never wait for smooth water, which never was and never will be, but, with what straggling method he can, dash with all his derangements at his object, leaving the rest to Fortune. (*Israel Potter* [London 1923] 151)

This is the guiding theme of *Israel Potter.* Israel plunges into one desperate action after another. Each time the universe is too much for him. Each time he falls back in pathetic defeat. The theme is not new. The Enceladus dream of *Pierre* announced it with less emotional restraint, but *Israel Potter* is written under the aegis of the same cosmic protest as *Pierre.* The Titan figure recurs

repeatedly in the later book, and London, like New York, is referred to as the
City of Dis.

There are, however, subtler parallels as well. Chapter I of *Israel Potter* is
written in the manner of Melville's best late prose. It is measured, intense,
suggestive, and symbolic. Melville's first sentence is deceptively casual, but it
openly announces that a particular kind of traveler, one who eschews the
locomotive and stage for the more leisurely pace of his own two legs, "will
find ample food for poetic reflection in the singular scenery of a country, which
owing to the ruggedness of the soil and its lying out of the track of all public
conveyances, remains almost as unknown to the general tourist as the interior
of Bohemia." What follows is a description of that same New England
mountain landscape that appeared in *Pierre,* but here done with the measured
suggestiveness of Melville's scenic descriptions in "The Encantadas" and "The
Piazza."

Melville notes the remains of the dwellings of those first settlers who clung
to the highlands to escape the miasmas of the lower valleys. The size of their
buildings and the rocks they used compel him to the same mythic reference
he used in *Pierre:*

> The very Titans seemed to have been at work. That so small an army
> as the first settlers must needs have been should have taken such wonder-
> ful pains to enclose so ungrateful a soil; that they should have accom-
> plished such herculean undertakings with so slight prospect of reward;
> this is a consideration which gives us a significant hint of the temper of
> the men of the Revolutionary era. (p 3)

Israel Potter is of such a temper. So are John Paul Jones and Ethan Allen. Titans
all.

In one respect this first chapter is the obverse of scenic description in *The
Encantadas.* There Melville focussed his attention on the signs of life and beauty
in a landscape appropriate only for death. Here the Berkshires are redolent of
summer blossoms and greenery, but everywhere there are grim reminders. One
might see a hawk "suddenly beset by a crow, who with stubborn audacity pecks
at him, and spite of all his bravery, finally persecutes him back to his strong-
hold. The otherwise dauntless bandit, soaring at his topmost height, must
needs succumb to this sable image of death" (p 4). Or the traveler "sees some
ghost-like object looming through the mist at the roadside; and wending
towards it, beholds a rude white stone, uncouthly inscribed, marking the spot
where, some fifty or sixty years ago, some farmer was upset in his woodsled,
and perished beneath the load" (p 5). Amid images of natural life and beauty
are carefully interspersed reminders of death just as in *Pierre* the Delectable
Mountain carries the baneful amaranth and in "The Piazza" the starry bloom
of the Chinese creeper carried "millions of strange, cankerous worms" within
its blossoms.

This is particularly the country in which Israel is born, but it is also the
world in which he is doomed to wander. The New England landscape becomes

a microcosm. Here is the "organic disorder" to which all human affairs are subject; here the "half-disciplined chaos" in which human affairs are created and sustained. "Such, at this day, is the country which gave birth to our hero: prophetically styled Israel by the good Puritans, his parents: since, for more than forty years, poor Potter wandered in the wild wilderness of the world's extremest hardships and ills" (p 5). The Titan Israel is doomed in the remainder of the novel consistently to "dash with all his derangements at his object, leaving the rest to Fortune!"

Constance Rourke [author of *American Humor*] could well have used Israel Potter as Exhibit A for the archetypal figure of the Yankee peddler. After the first chapter Israel is quickly described as farmer, hunter, trapper, soldier, sailor; and he literally peddled goods to the Indians, thus acquiring "that fearless self-reliance and independence which conducted our forefathers to national freedom" (p 10). This undoubtedly was one of the reasons for Melville's interest in the tale of this pathetic soldier of the Revolution. Israel Potter was a ready-made American archetype whose name suggested a Biblical parallel attractive to Melville's dark view of his contemporary world. It only remained for Melville to link him to the Titan figure described insistently in *Pierre* for Israel to take on the dimensions peculiar to Melville's fiction.

However, the first important character of American history whom Israel meets contrasts sharply with the Titan figure. Benjamin Franklin is a cross between Plotinus Plinlimmon of *Pierre* and the bland moralistic Confidence Man. Pierre, the moral Titan who rages at the wickedness and callousness of the world about him, is baffled and repulsed by the nonbenevolence of Plotinus Plinlimmon. Similarly, but in a more comic vein, Israel is consistently baffled by the remoteness and worldly prudence of Franklin. Potter's outburst after Franklin "protects" him from the chamber-maid is humorously just, "Every time he comes in he robs me." The Missouri bachelor, another Titan figure, is likewise robbed and befuddled by the worldliness and insincerity of the Confidence Man.

Franklin and John Paul Jones, who appears shortly after Israel meets Franklin, are complements. Melville describes Franklin with light but sharp irony:

> Having carefully weighed the world, Franklin could act in any part of it. By nature turned to knowledge, his mind was often grave, but never serious. At times he had seriousness—extreme seriousness—for others, but never for himself. Tranquility was to him instead of it. . . . Jack of all trades, master of each and mastered by none—the type and genius of his land. Franklin was everything but a poet. (p 62)

John Paul Jones on the other hand has something in him of the poet as well as the outlaw. He is intensely serious, though seldom grave. He is restless and impetuous, never tranquil. And if in this book Melville seems at one point to fear that America may yet become the John Paul Jones of nations, in *The Confidence Man* he seems to find it far more likely that America will become the Benjamin Franklin of nations. "Poor Richard's Almanac," or "Way to

Wealth," which takes a practical and prudent look at man's world and suggests a code of behavior based on self-interest—just as did [Plinlimmon's] "Chronometricals and Horologicals"—is juxtaposed in Melville's view to the Bible which speaks poetry, terrible mystery, and compassion.

Thus there is a fine dramatic irony in John Paul Jones' captaining a vessel named the *Bon Homme Richard* and paying lip service to such moralisms as "God helps them that help themselves" from the Almanac. It is a little like Huckleberry Finn's admiration for Tom Sawyer. In effect Jones does not believe that God helps them that help themselves. His is a more poetically complicated feeling toward the universe and his part in it or he would never have been so awed by that "cock of the walk of the sea . . . yon Crag of Ailsa." Like Huck he knows intuitively the awesome mystery of the natural universe. He is not presumptuous with God, only with civilization. . . .

The engagement between the *Bon Homme Richard* and the *Serapis* is the climax of *Israel Potter*. Significantly enough it was "luck" that "shortly threw in Paul's way the great action of his life." But for Melville the engagement is more than simply a chance occurrence. It is a potential prophecy: "Sharing the blood with England, and yet her proved foe in two wars—not wholly inclined at bottom to forget an old grudge—intrepid, unprincipled, reckless, predatory, with boundless ambition, civilized in externals but a savage at heart, America is, or may yet be, the Paul Jones of nations" (158). The battle is between savage intrepidity and civilization and its traditions. It is fought under a full harvest moon before a part of the English coast that suggests the primal desolation of the Encantadas: "Here and there the base of the cliffs is strewn with masses of rock, undermined by the waves, and tumbled headlong below, where, sometimes, the water completely surrounds them, showing in shattered confusion detached rocks, pyramids, and obelisks, rising half-revealed from the surf—the Tadmores of the wasteful desert of the sea" (159).

The *Richard* is manned by a "motley crew" and carries a "hybrid band" of soldiers. Its "armament was similarly heterogeneous." That microcosm of American democracy, the *Pequod* [in *Moby-Dick*], comes readily to mind. Because the sea allows for none of the devious stratagems of land warfare—such as ambuscades—the battle is "more akin to the Miltonic contests of archangels than to *the comparatively squalid* tussles of earth" (161). But the battle takes place in the evening, and if the sea demands open warfare, the evening mist lends sufficient ambiguity to the scene to tempt Melville's ironic and poetic talents. He describes a harvest moon premonitory of the baleful significance of Doctor T. J. Eckleburg [in *The Great Gatsby*] looking over the valley of ashes:

> Not long after, an invisible hand came and set down a great yellow lamp in the east. The hand reached up unseen from below the horizon, and set the lamp down right on the rim of the horizon, as on a threshold. . . . The lamp was the round harvest moon; the one solitary footlight of the scene. But scarcely did the rays from the lamp pierce that languid haze. Objects before perceived with difficulty, now glimmered ambiguously. Bedded in strange vapors, the great footlight cast a dubious, half demoniac

glare across the waters, like the phantasmagoric stream sent athwart a London flagging in a night-rain from an apothecary's blue and green window. Through this sardonical mist, the face of the Man-in-the-Moon—looking right towards the combatants, as if he were standing in a trapdoor of the sea, leaning forward leisurely with his arms complacently folded over upon the edge of the horizon—this queer face wore a serious, apishly self-satisfied leer, as if the Man-in-the-Moon had somehow secretly put up the ships to their contest, and in the depths of his malignant old soul was not unpleased to see how well his charms worked. There stood the grinning Man-in-the-Moon,—Mephistopheles prompter of the stage. (162-163)

Finally through chance and Israel's quick action the ships are bound together cheek by jowl with only a few feet of dark threatening water between them. The terrible fratricidal nature of a war between America and Britain is again reflected in the image the two ships present: "It seemed more an intestine feud, than a fight between strangers. Or, rather, it was as if the Siamese Twins, oblivious of their fraternal bond, should rage in unnatural fight" (165). The heavier and more efficient cannon of the *Serapis* clears the men from the *Richard's* covered gundeck. On the other hand the superior musketry of the *Richard* clears the upper deck of the *Serapis*. "It was a co-partnership and joint-stock combustion-company of both ships; yet divided, even in participation" (167).

Israel drops a grenade into the bowels of the *Serapis*. The *Richard* is unaccountably attacked by her own sister ship the *Alliance*. It is at this point that the English Captain asks Jones if he strikes and gains the famous answer, "I have not yet begun to fight." But all is confusion. Officers of the *Richard* shout for quarter. The English prisoners escape from the hold of the *Richard*, but it proves a blessing in disguise as they are quickly put to work manning the pumps. The fighting now goes in favor of the *Richard*, but Melville's description of the surrender of the *Serapis* indicates there is some question of who is the true victor: "Mutual obliteration from the face of the waters seemed the only natural sequel to hostilities like these. It is, therefore, honor to him as a man, and not reproach to him as an officer, that, to stay such carnage, Captain Pearson, of the *Serapis* with his own hands hauled down his colors" (172).

Captain Pearson was less the savage than John Paul Jones. His surrender is represented by Melville as an act of humanity. But the carnage is not complete even then. After the surrender the *Richard* is gutted by flames, and late that evening "the *Richard*, gorged with slaughter, wallowed heavily, gave a long roll, and blasted by tornadoes of sulphur, slowly sank, like Gomorrah, out of sight" (173). Melville closes the battle with a question related to the prophecy of the beginning: "In view of this battle one may ask—What separates the enlightened man from the savage? Is civilization a thing distinct, or is it an advanced stage of barbarism?" (173). Melville has asked this question in many forms since the writing of *Typee*. But he has never before made it the basis of pathetic comedy. The individual Titan is so dwarfed by the complex irrationalities of both civilization and nature that the reader can only smile sympathetically at man's attempt to assert his humanity. Melville, like Henry Adams, builds an ironic tension between what his sensitive moral nature demands man and his civilization to be and what he finds them to be.

Jones is a heroic figure, but he is not ideal. He is vainglorious and barbaric, but his faults are called for by his time. The arrogant naval cruelties of the British—the impressment of American seamen and the raids on the American coast—had to be answered. Barbarism is warranted, but barbarism paradoxically denies the humanity it strives to assert. In this Jones represents America. He is part of a cosmic morality play whose issue is still shrouded in moral confusion. Can America find her way to meaningful civilization? Will the world situation permit her to drop her puerile aggressiveness? Or will the need for a stable and respected position in the world community force her to deny her innocence and faith and adapt the worldly opportunism of Benjamin Franklin? Melville can see no clear cut answer to these questions, but all the signs are ominous.

After this climactic battle and again through the agency of chance Israel finds himself abandoned aboard an English ship fleeing an engagement with the *Ariel* newly commanded by John Paul Jones. Israel tries to masquerade as a member of the crew, but he cannot impose upon any of the bands of sailors. Finally he feigns madness. In an alien world man pretends what he is not, so that he will not be destroyed. Israel has been forced to disguise on numerous occasions in the past and so long as the state of the world is war the necessity will still be with him. Thus when he returns to England and encounters Ethan Allen imprisoned, his own relative freedom is partly illusory. As Melville reminds us by a chapter heading, Israel is in Egypt.

Ethan Allen is another American Titan. He is a wild man, but he is more essentially human than the stuffy and cowardly representatives of civilization that surround him. He has heart and extravagance in contrast to the priggish narrow-mindedness of the crowds that gape at him. He receives some kindnesses from the people who visit him, but these are the exceptions rather than the rule. He exists in a hostile world that justifies his Titanism.

From this point on Israel's career is rapidly brought to its pathetic close. The war, hard times, family responsibilities, and illnesses deprive him of any possibility of realizing his dream of returning to his native land until he and that land through long estrangement have grown foreign to one another. He carries on his pathetic battle to exist, unable to order his life because of the organic disorder of the world in which he lives. He is an American in a foreign country, but as Melville describes the country in which Israel was born, it too is a wilderness discouraging to civilization and humanity. Israel's struggle is the struggle of man to control his fate and it reflects the problem of America to realize her destiny.

Between *Pierre* and *The Confidence Man* there is a noticeable withdrawal of the author's personal commentary. *Pierre* is painful because Melville is too personally involved in his story. In *The Confidence Man,* on the other hand, Melville has so completely hidden his self behind ambiguously ironic incident and a tautly controlled prose that one has difficulty finding any norm, whether of narrative, ideal, or character, by which to judge the action of the story. *Israel Potter* helps explain the movement between the two novels. Melville's personal emotions are under more conscious control in *Israel Potter* than in *Pierre*. The Titanism of Pierre is examined with more controlled objectivity in the figures of Jones, Allen, and Potter himself. Plotinus Plinlimmon's representation of prudential self-interest, which is in opposition to Titanism, is more fully elaborated in the character of Benjamin Franklin. All are finally viewed in the baleful moonlight of pathetic comedy.

From *"Israel Potter:* Pathetic Comedy," *Bulletin of the New York Public Library,* 65 (Feb. 1961), 125-32.

CHARLES G. HOFFMANN

The Shorter Fiction of Herman Melville

[In addition to the works discussed below, this essay treats others such as "Cock-A-Doodle-Doo!" and *The Encantadas,* on the thesis that Melville turned to shorter fiction after the difficulties of trying to unify "large blocks of material," recalcitrant material, in *Moby-Dick* and *Pierre.*]

In *Bartleby the Scrivener* are two evidences of Melville's artistic control over his material, clear from the beginning even before Bartleby himself is introduced: (1) the concrete, realistic background of the law office and (2) the character of the narrator from whose point of view the story is told. The law office, in which most of the action takes place, is realistically described; Melville creates a suggestive atmosphere of confinement and isolation, of a well-ordered and insulated world the boundaries of which are clearly defined. Into this dismally dull but eminently safe world Bartleby enters.

The character of the narrator, the lawyer who maintains these offices and who hires Bartleby, is carefully built up from the beginning. He is no Ahab or Pierre who risks all in a titanic struggle; he is not even an ambitious lawyer pleading a cause with the applause of the public. He is a lawyer who "in the cool tranquility of a snug retreat," does a "snug business among rich men's bonds and mortgages and title-deeds. All who know me, consider me an eminently *safe* man." Prudence and method are his strong points. Through the years he has learned to be patient with others, as can be seen in his acceptance of the eccentricities of his two copyists, Turkey and Nippers. The eccentric behavior of Turkey and Nippers forms a balance that does not disrupt the more or less smooth working of the business; indeed their behavior becomes part of the ordered pattern of life in the world of the law offices. In this ordered world among these men of habit Bartleby appears, "pallidly neat, pitiably respectable, incurably forlorn."

Five words, "I would prefer not to," uttered mildly and firmly but without any note of defiance, threaten the whole structure of the world. The employer is helpless in the face of Bartleby's passive resistance to duty, method, and order. The employer, the narrator, can of course fire Bartleby on the spot; he is Authority, to whom the scriveners owe obedience. But to fire Bartleby, as he later discovers, does not rid him of Bartleby's presence and the enigmatic problem of his preferring not to. Those words become a refrain, repeated by Bartleby at every request for compliance; they become the epitaph of nonconformity. Bartleby is kept on in spite of his unwillingness to conform. The employer finds some excuse to postpone the inevitable crisis—his work is too pressing, he wishes to give Bartleby time to think things over, he hopes that either the crisis will go away and Bartleby will become reasonable or that Bartleby will go away of his own accord. But Bartleby does not change; he continues to prefer not to even to the point of not doing any work.

The employer is confounded by the irrationality of Bartleby's behavior. Being a rational man and living in a rationally ordered world, he cannot understand the irrational. Irony underscores his efforts to find a rational reason for Bartleby's preferring not to: perhaps his eyes are weak, and he needs to rest them. Irony underlies his attempts to explain the rationale of why Bartleby ought to do what he prefers not to. Traditionalism in the form of obedience and duty, utilitarianism in the form of usefulness and methodology, self-interest in the form of ambition and survival: this is the rationale of the world into which Bartleby has entered. But it is a rationale that can be destroyed by the irrational element in the universe.

True, both Turkey and Nippers at times exhibit irrational behavior, but their irrationalism never destroys their conformity; they do their duty in the prescribed way at all times despite minor rumblings of dissent, and their irrational behavior follows a pattern that becomes part of the regularity and order rather than an uncontrolled element outside. In contrast, Bartleby's irrationalism is inscrutable; it is the element of mystery in the world, against which all reason is helpless. It is there; it cannot be explained away; there is no escape from it. Something of this the narrator intuitively recognizes in postponing a "settlement" with Bartleby, in his growing sense of fear and anxiety, and his attempt to escape by moving to a different location. Yet he cannot help feeling sympathy for Bartleby; his friendlessness, loneliness, solitude, and terrible isolation are a melancholy and pitiful sight. Bartleby is an outcast in a utilitarian world; like Hawthorne's Wakefield, he has stepped outside the system to which the world is adjusted and thus has lost his place forever.

In this story Melville achieves complexity through simplicity and economy. He has completely reversed the method of *Moby-Dick* and *Pierre,* in which, particularly in the latter, he sought to achieve complexity through elaboration and expansion of rhetoric. . . .

Bartleby the Scrivener is not, however, a flawless work of art. The point of view is consistently maintained, the action structurally inclosed, the atmosphere and tone sustained throughout. Even the shift of the scene of the action from the inclosed world of the law offices, which provides much of the underlying meaning of the story, to the outside world is a consistent and logical consequence of the situation. The narrator hopes to escape from Bartleby, whose presence seems like some inescapable fate, as though to remove himself from Bartleby's presence would remove that fate. Bartleby's removal to prison, ordered by the new occupant of the offices, is part of the theme that one must be useful in this society or be cast out by it. The prison itself is but another isolated world reflecting the prison of life. The final long paragraph is the flaw that mars the perfection of the whole. Melville did not let well enough alone. The ending is anticlimactic. It is a flaw because it takes the reader outside the confines of the story itself; it attempts to add biographical information about

Bartleby after enough has been said. Worse still, the artistic purpose of the ending, a metaphorical summing up of Bartleby's life, falls flat. Melville expands the rumor that Bartleby had been a subordinate clerk in the Dead Letter Office at Washington into a metaphor to signify his hopeless life. This information is consistent within the point of view, but is out of tone with the rest of the story and its meaning. The metaphor is more of a play on words than an adequate summary of the meaning of the story, a pun rather than a symbol. . . .

"The Lightning-Rod Man" and "The Happy Failure" continue Melville's satiric attack on commercialism. The satire in the latter story (published in *Harper's Magazine,* July, 1854) is incidental to the ironic anecdote of the man who spends ten years enslaved to his invention, a machine for draining marsh-land, only to find happiness and freedom in the failure of the machine to work. In the former story the satire is direct: a lightning-rod salesman cringes at the sound of thunder and yet offers for profit freedom from fear of lightning in the form of the lightning rod. Coming in the middle of a lightning storm, he preys upon the fears of others, hoping that the nearness of the storm will increase his sales. The ineffectiveness of man's efforts to free himself from natural dangers is seen in the fear-ridden life of the lightning-rod man in contrast with the dignity of the narrator, who recognizes nature's power and takes his chances without fear. It is seen also in the contrast between the destructiveness of the lightning bolt and the seeming impossibility that a short length of metal rod should channel that destructive power. The lightning rod, symbol of man's progress against nature, seems a puny thing to guard against being struck by lightning, the Biblical symbol of God's wrath. This successful balance and contrast of symbols make "The Lightning-Rod Man" one of Melville's best short stories.

Melville's source for *Benito Cereno* was Captain Delano's *Narrative of Voyages and Travels, in the Northern and Southern Hemispheres* together with the legal documents of the investigation and trial. The strange events had happened, and the source of information was an eyewitness account by Captain Delano himself. Though Melville follows closely enough the true account and though he includes unchanged except for minor deletions portions of the testimony, the novel is not merely a transcription of the source. Delano's narrative is a factual account of what actually happened. The strangeness and excitement of the actual events were sufficient in themselves for an unembellished, straight-forward account; Melville, using this account as a source, could not add very much to the basic narrative without sacrificing plausibility. Indeed, so far as narrative interest is concerned, the adventures described by Delano are suffi-cient to make an interesting and exciting story. But *Benito Cereno* is much more than an adventure story about pirating, mutiny, and rescue on the high seas. The suspense that hints at impending evil and casts an ambiguous light on past incidents, Captain Delano's suspicions of the presence of evil for which he can find no explanation, the isolation and fear of Benito Cereno, who is helpless to speak out against his captor—these are the means by which Melville transforms a true account into a work of art.

A key to Melville's achievement in *Benito Cereno* is the portrayal of Captain Delano himself. From Delano's own account we get an impression that, as Professor Thorp suggests, he is "a brave, conscientious, and resourceful commander whose nerves are unaffected by experiences aboard the *Tryal* and whose main concern is the capture of the ship as a valuable prize, after Don Benito has given her up for lost." In the novel Captain Delano, while brave and resourceful, is prone to speculation, doubts, and suspicions stimulated by the contradictory behavior of Benito Cereno; his main concern is to fathom the mystery surrounding Cereno's extraordinary behavior and the ambiguous incidents that take place. Delano's point of view is central in the novel. Melville did not reconstruct the events that led up to the mutiny and the imprisonment of the Spaniards by the Negroes. Instead, he limited himself to the climactic events leading to the rescue of Benito Cereno and his crew; for dramatic intensity, concentrated action, and structural unity no better choice could have been made. Melville concentrated on those events in which Delano took part. Since his artistic purpose was not merely to tell a story of adventure but also to create an atmosphere of evil and mystery eventually revealed in all its horror, the establishment of the point of view from which the story is told is important to the successful achievement of that purpose.

First, Delano, being an outsider, knows nothing of the real situation on board the *San Dominick*. His is the "innocent eye" on which impressions are made by what he sees much as they are on James's governess in *The Turn of the Screw*. Furthermore, Captain Delano is characterized as "a person of a singularly undistrustful good nature." So trustful is his nature that he is "not liable, except on extraordinary and repeated excitement, and hardly then, to indulge in personal alarms, any way involving the imputation of malign evil in man." This trustfulness is important in the light of later events, particularly Delano's habit of dismissing doubts and suspicions as being fanciful and unreal when a man of suspicious nature would be thoroughly convinced of the evil present on board the ship.

Something is amiss. Even the sea reflects the suspense and atmosphere of hidden mystery. The strange ship that comes into view displays no flag, although it is the custom of all peaceful ships to show their colors. On closer view the neglect and disorder on board the *San Dominick* in contrast with the neatness and order on Delano's ship are evidence of laxity or weakness of authority, hinting that catastrophe had overcome its officers. The carved stern piece dominated by the figure of a masked satyr pinioning with his foot another masked figure suggests hidden mystery. This figure is of course the symbol of Babo's mastery over the weak and frightened Cereno. They are masked, since ostensibly Babo is Cereno's servant; he plays the role to delude Delano and ward off suspicions and yet have a legitimate reason for staying close to Cereno at all times. The masking also suggests Delano's inability to see through Babo's masquerade; until Babo attacks Cereno in the whale boat, Delano directs all his suspicions and doubts toward Cereno. Only with that act of violence is Babo's mask ripped off and his villainy revealed. . . .

The style of *Benito Cereno* is straightforward in its simplicity and objectivity, and economical in its brevity and clarity. But it is not barren or lacking in complex effects. It might be supposed that the unadorned, straightforward account of the source had some influence on the style of Melville's *Benito Cereno.* But it did not except in Melville's deliberate retention of the legalistic, dry tone of the extracts from the trial documents—for purposes of verisimilitude and separation from the main narrative. Actually, one of the major differences between the source and the novel, the difference that makes the one a factual account and the other an artistic account, is the stylistic means by which Melville transforms a matter-of-fact narrative into an imaginative creation.

Though not perfect in itself, the style is a far cry from the exaggerated and derivative rhetoric of *Pierre.* This development toward a simpler, less flamboyant prose style is by no means first observable in *Benito Cereno.* The simplicity of the style in *Bartleby the Scrivener* has been noted. In contrast to the style of *Moby-Dick* and *Pierre,* the style of Melville's works both before and after is on the whole natural in idiom rather than flowery, suggestive in imagery rather than flamboyant, personal rather than derivative. . . .

From "The Shorter Fiction of Herman Melville," *The South Atlantic Quarterly,* 52 (July 1953), 414-30.

PAUL McCARTHY

The "Soldier of Fortune"
in Melville's *The Confidence Man*

WHILE MANY critics have commented briefly upon the significance of the
crippled "soldier" in *The Confidence-Man*, few have discussed him at any
length.[1] He is clearly a minor figure, another con man working his wiles upon
the gullibility and charity of passengers aboard the steamer *Fidèle*. One of eight
"ge'mmen" referred to by the Negro cripple, he is no Satanic confidence man,
but a disciple of the Devil.[2] The purpose of this paper is to show the extent
to which the "Soldier of Fortune" is under the Devil's tutelage.

From the beginning of their meeting, which is described in Chapter XIX,
the herb-doctor is aware of the cripple's actual nature and purpose. Possessing
supernatural powers, the herb-doctor would instantly recognize anyone who
had taken up his own nefarious calling. The cripple's reply of " 'Resaca de la
Tombs,' " his tattered and suspicious appearance, and his "half moody, half
surly" manner, point to a dubious past. He morosely admits that he is not a
modern Lazarus risen from the dead, but a Lazarus "with sores," a beggar.
Taken aback by such cynicism, the friendly herb-doctor asks him to show
confidence and also tell how he has arrived at such misfortune. At this point
the cripple, grasping the identity of the individual before him, stares with the
"hard ironic eye of one toughened and defiant in misery, and, in the end,
grinned upon him with his unshaven face like an ogre" (p. 106). The herb-
doctor calls upon him to be "human. . . . Don't make that face; it distresses
me'." (*Ibid.*) The cripple, in other words, should not try to be a monster or a
fiendish con man: he is only a human con man and a rather ordinary one at
that, if one not easily put upon. " 'I suppose,' (he said) with a sneer, 'you are
the man I've long heard of—The Happy Man'." (*Ibid.*) The "soldier" is far from
pleased because his relationship with the confidence man has not been happy;
it has resulted in his paralyzed legs and lowly status. He angrily admits that
for some time he has longed to get hold of The Happy Man, fill him with
powder, and let him explode " 'at his leisure.' " No raw recruit in the regiment
of the criminal and damned, the cripple knows what he is dealing with. He
proceeds to air his troubles and, at the same time, re-enlighten the herb-doctor
about details of his own past.

The resulting story-within-a-story serves a vital function in the meeting by

1. See *The Confidence-Man: His Masquerade*, ed. Elizabeth S. Foster (N.Y., 1954), pp. lxx-lxxi.
Subsequent references to this edition will appear in the text. For another discussion of the cripple,
see James E. Miller, Jr., *"The Confidence-Man*: His Guises," *PMLA*, LXXIV, 107 (March, 1959).
2. *Ibid.*

revealing the cripple's earliest relationship with the con man. The story begins with an account of the strange fight between a sober pavior and a gentleman who had been drinking. Despite his great strength, the pavior was quickly dispatched by a sword thrust. When the herb-doctor, very likely feigning ignorance, inquires " 'How was that?' " the cripple explains, " 'Why you see the pavior undertook something above his strength'." (p. 107) The phrase "undertook something above his strength" is repeated in three consecutive sentences by the cripple. This curious phrase, about which the herb-doctor ironically appears in doubt, certainly refers to someone or something with unusual and mysterious powers. It is as if the herb-doctor wants his disciple to come right out and state the identity of the gentleman, but the disciple will not. He continues with his story, leaving the implication that the gentleman successful at the fight and later at the trial is none other than the Devil himself, once again masquerading to deceive mankind.

The gentleman confidence man, according to the cripple, was not only acquitted of his crime, but presented with a gold watch and chain by admiring friends. In contrast the "soldier," unaware then of the con man's identity and of the folly of testifying against him, met with misfortune. He was kept in prison because he lacked money, and he lacked money because he had no friends.

By leading to further disclosures of the cripple's past, the herb-doctor's seemingly innocuous questions underline a basic truth for the cripple. Ability to make friends is highly prized by all confidence men, for how otherwise could they begin to deceive potential victims? In commenting upon the astonishing acquittal, the herb-doctor remarks, " 'If this speak prosaically for justice, it speaks romantically for friendship' "! (p. 109) Only in the Devil's first appearance aboard the *Fidèle* as the man in cream-colors is he without friends, and then his masquerade serves to explain his loneliness. In other disguises he is never without at least one friendly listener. Another incident in the cripple's story supports the fact that past misfortune was due primarily to lack of friendly assistance. Having developed bone troubles from his confinement in the wet cell, the cripple had no other place to go than a government hospital where he spent three years, all because he had no friends. Since that time he has been a member of the " 'Devil's regiment.' " If honesty will not pay, perhaps deception will.

But, as his account so plainly reveals, the cripple has failed to prove himself as a disciple of the con man: he lacks the artfulness necessary to consistently overcome the defenses of prospective victims. When he completes the story, the herb-doctor remarks, " 'You must pardon me, if I honestly tell you, I cannot believe it'." (p. 110) The herb-doctor does not doubt the story because he defends it from attacks by a "prim-looking stranger," who questions the cripple's veracity. Referring to the stories of the Tombs and military service, the herb-doctor explains, " 'Though the inglorious lock-jaw of his knee-pans in a wet dungeon is a far more pitiable ill than to have been crippled at glorious Contreras, yet he is of opinion that this lighter and false ill shall attract, while the heavier and real one might repel'." (*Ibid.*) The herb-doctor's criticism is not of truth or falsehood, but of method. He is displeased with a story too grim to elicit either sympathy or envy from a listener. Optimistic as he is in most cases, the herb-doctor would never tell such a gloomy story, but inveigle his listener with something intriguing and artful. The cripple is not unaware of the defects of his story; he soon wanders down the deck of the *Fidèle* with another tale with which to hoodwink his fellow passengers. This " 'lighter and false ill' " about alleged war experiences at Buena Vista results in "a pretty good harvest" because the cripple adopts a friendly manner and pleasant tone. He may yet develop into a successful and adroit con man.

Under the discerning eye of the master deceiver still another flaw becomes evident in the *modus operandi* of the tattered disciple. He is sarcastically critical of America or " 'free Ameriky,' " as he calls it. Whatever doubts the herb-doctor may have about freedom, opportunity, and justice in America, he keeps them to himself. Nor will he allow a disciple to criticize the country in which he operates. He questions the cripple's lack of patriotism and gratitude: whatever difficulties he may have endured under the government, his morose reflections are unwarranted. The con man ironically explains that one must have confidence in both earthly and heavenly law even though both at times may appear unfair or unequal in their operations. " 'Nevertheless, to one who has a right confidence, final benignity is, in every instance, as sure with the one law as the other'." (p. 111) To help convince the unsuspecting that he is worthy of trust, the con man must appear to have a high faith in the laws of man and of God.

Disillusioned and skeptical, the cripple is not to be won by idealistic palaver. " 'What do you talk your hog-latin to me for' "? he cries. (p. 112) When the con man refers to transformations wrought by charity, the soldier replies sarcastically that people should not be chastened too much, for then their hearts would harden and feel neither pain nor joy. When the con man speaks of living fully and partaking of the glorious air and sun and of skipping about for joy, the cripple replies that he cannot skip about on legs that are "horse-posts." Such reactions bring the herb-doctor back to " 'my original object' " which is to gain confidence and give assistance. He thus proceeds to "assist" his disciple.

Alike in that both are deceivers, the herb-doctor and the crippled "soldier" differ in that one is the master deceiver and the other is merely a pupil or disciple. One will teach in his own unique manner and the other must learn if he is to prosper. As the cripple is too inexperienced or cynical to learn by irony and verbal play, he must learn from practical example.

The example is that he, too, like others aboard the steamer *Fidèle,* must be victimized by schemes of the master deceiver. Because of the cripple's arrogant skepticism and his obvious faults as a confidence man, he must pay a penalty. Ironically, he falls prey to the very technique advocated by the herb-doctor throughout much of their meeting: friendliness. The relationship of the two men, then, is not merely that of master instructing pupil, but also that of deceiver fleecing victim. To accomplish his object, the con man must first gain his victim's confidence. He does so by asking nothing from him and by doing for him what he had allegedly done earlier for the Negro cripple. " 'His case was a little something like yours,' " the herb-doctor remarks. (*Ibid.*) He tells the human cripple that " 'I will not force confidence on you. Still, I would fain do the friendly thing by you. Here, take the box. . . . Take it. Nothing to pay. God bless you. Good-bye'." (p. 113) Kind words and reassuring manners gradually weaken the cripple's skepticism until he believes that the herb-doctor is treating him as a real friend. This must be so, he thinks, because the herb-doctor asks for nothing in return. He even persists upon leaving without payment. Before the con man departs, the cripple relents completely and offers to pay for the boxes. But the confidence man will accept nothing whatsoever, at least not at first. He explains that he has been amply rewarded by the rebirth of "confidence and hopefulness," excellent qualities which will aid the cripple as much as crutches aid him. That anyone can show such faith and confidence in him proves to be too much for the cripple, who humbly remarks, " 'You have made a better man of me. You have borne with me like a good Christian, and talked to me like one, and all that is enough without making me a present of these boxes. Here is the money. I won't take nay'." (*Ibid.*)

The circle is completed; the entrapment is finished. On this April First aboard the steamer *Fidèle,* the cripple proves to be less shrewd a skeptic than the Missouri Bachelor and less practiced a schemer than Charles Noble. What specific points the cripple will have gained from the encounter cannot be said. That the encounter will make him more disillusioned toward his master is certain. That it will also make him more determined to outwit his fellow man is hardly less certain. Thus, as the herb-doctor walks down the deck with the money, the cripple may be no more a victim than he is a pupil. He will henceforth be more alert when the Devil is around. And because the "soldier" is pragmatic and shrewd he may recover from his duping soon enough to practice what, in effect, the Devil has preached; he may even fleece another victim or two before midnight comes. At least it can be expected that on some future day aboard the *Fidèle* the "Soldier of Fortune" will appear as a knowledgeable con man with skills and devices more to the Devil's liking.

From "The 'Soldier of Fortune' in Melville's *The Confidence Man*," *The Emerson Society Quarterly,* No. 33 (1963), pp. 21-24.

RICHARD HARTER FOGLE

The Themes of Melville's Later Poetry

IN HIS long poem *Clarel* [1876] Melville consistently reverts to the sea for metaphor and illustration. The small lattices of Clarel's inn look down on the Pool of Hezekiah

> As a three-decker's stern-lights peer
> Down on the oily wake below . . . ;
>
> (I, 7)

the Illinois prairie of Nathan's boyhood is like the ocean in

> Long rollings of the vast serene—
> The prairie in her swimming swell
> Of undulation.
>
> (I, 70)

An unfriendly rabbi, discouraging Clarel from Ruth's acquaintance, "Sat a torpedo-fish with mind/Intent to paralyze," (I, 96) a figure which was used more notably in *Billy Budd* many years later to describe the villain Claggart's hypnotic eyes. . . . These are a few examples out of many: the desert is like the ocean, science is a light-ship among shoals, the thought of Ruth to Clarel on the pilgrimage is like a ship fading in the distance.

Significantly, too, Melville resorts to the sea for the background of his "devotees," perhaps his favorite characters, men who have been tried and almost broken, who have learned to accept the burden of life with patience, humility, and—in some fortunate cases—faith. Rolfe, the writer's self-portrait, looks wistfully back to his adventurous youth, even as "A truant ship-boy overworn" (II, 140). The saint Nehemiah's past is clouded, but one version of it makes him an over-confident ship-captain broken in to the truth by a series of disasters. The fullest association with the sea, however, comes through the elderly timoneer, a mild ancient mariner whom the pilgrims encounter at the monastery of Mar Saba. He has connections in his past experience with the story of Jonah, and in the same tale ("The Timoneer's Story," II, 58f.) with the reversed-compasses theme which Melville had touched upon in *Moby Dick* and was to take up twice more in "The Haglets" and "The Admiral of the White." Except in *Moby Dick* the erring compasses lead directly to shipwreck on a lee shore. The timoneer's adventures are always chastening and usually ominous. He preludes the strange loss of Mortmain's skull-cap with his tale of "Man and Bird," (II, 129f.), and in his account of "The Island" he draws a specific parallel between Palestine and the hellish Galapagos or "Encantadas."

The great tortoise of the Encantadas is a symbol of helpless subjection to chance, time, and fate. Melville associates him with the patient timoneer himself, and with the long-suffering donkey of Palestine and the Levant, but because of his size, his reptilian strangeness, and his incredible longevity the tortoise is most impressive of the three, and most horrible. He is an almost-eternal sufferer. . . .

John Marr and other Sailors (1888) portrays another of Melville's devotees as title-character, and like *Clarel* it links the sea and the land. John Marr is an old sailor, in peaceful but lonely exile in the ocean-like prairies of the Illinois of the 1830's. Like other Melville victims of fate, he is caught by life and inescapably fixed; his wife and family, for whom he left the sea, are dead, and the farmers among whom he dwells can give him little sympathy or under-standing. The poems of *John Marr* are songs of exile from another place and time, expressions of irremediable melancholy and loss. At the same time, there is a serenity in them not present in *Clarel* and other earlier works, a subtle and complex state of mind containing both peace and a sort of *horror vacui* imaged in the prairie itself, "the bed of a dried-up sea" where "Blank stillness would for hours reign unbroken." One would not stress the serenity too far above the bleak emptiness that goes with it. Very probably the tone of the *John Marr* poems accurately represents the dominant strain of the aging Melville, at once calmer and more hopeless than the doubt and sporadic violence of *Clarel.*

John Marr and other Sailors, a small collection of sea-pieces, is more consist-ent and aesthetically more satisfactory than *Battle-Pieces* [1866] or *Clarel,* per-haps because it is less ambitious and briefer. In it a more relaxed Melville turns to his past, now remote and idealized by long assimilative reflection. The themes of *John Marr* are traceable to earlier fiction and poetry of his, and some of them occur still later in *Billy Budd.* John Marr, the exiled sailor, resembles the earlier Israel Potter, who suffered a long Babylonian captivity. We have already noted the prairie-and-sea relationship, which goes back to *Clarel* and still further to *Moby Dick.* Marr wistfully recalls the childlike prelapsarian seamen of a vanished age,

> Barbarians of man's simpler nature,
> Unworldly servers of the world,

and these are to be found in all the earlier sea-novels—though not so clearly outlined—as well as the later *Billy Budd.* In natural proximity are celebrations of the heroes and the beautiful, poetic vessels of sail, before the naval Iron Age, such as can be found in *Battle-Pieces* and in *Billy Budd.* A pervasive nostalgia for the past is inseparable from these, as is the death-theme characteristic of Melville, and an historical and commemorative purpose most evident in *Battle-Pieces* among his earlier works. The indifference of nature in the cruel and capricious sea is an element in more than one poem; there are the devotees of fate, resembling Nehemiah and the timoneer of *Clarel;* and there is the heavy and ominous tread of doom, as in "The Scout toward Aldie" *(Battle-Pieces)* and of course most prominently in *Moby Dick.* "Bridegroom Dick," the longest of the John Marr poems, goes back directly to *White-Jacket,* with a significant change, however, in point of view. . . .

Timoleon (1891), like *John Marr and other Poems,* was printed in a tiny edition of twenty-five copies. Its poetry, for the most part the product of Melville's old age, is of even higher quality. As its title indicates, it has much to say of ancient Greece, its spirit, its art, and its law. From the Romantic organicism voiced in *Moby Dick* Melville now turns explicitly to admiration for classic restraint and finish, which he emulates in his verse. The change is not complete or absolute, and it is not sudden; but change it is, and in *Timoleon* for the first time unmistakably evident. A group of poems on art, "The Weaver," "In a Garret," "Art," "The Attic Landscape," "The Parthenon," "Greek Masonry," and "Greek Architecture" strike the note:

> Not magnitude, not lavishness,
> But Form—the Site:
> Not innovating wilfulness,
> But reverence for the Archetype.

("Greek Architecture")

It need not be felt that Melville in appreciating has wholly adopted the Grecian ideal; his poems are objective, dramatic, and tentative. Yet the emphasis is ineluctably significant.

On the evidence of *Timoleon,* Melville was seeking a synthesis rather than an exclusion in his altered theory of art. He appears to be tightening and supplementing organicism rather than banishing it. His most notable utterance, in fact, employs the organicist terminology, but with unusual concentration upon the *struggle* of artistic creation.

> In placid hours well-pleased we dream
> Of many a brave unbodied scheme,
> But form to lend, pulsed life create,
> What unlike things must meet and mate:
> A flame to melt—a wind to freeze;
> Sad patience—joyous energies;
> Humility—yet pride and scorn;
> Instinct and study; love and hate;
> Audacity—reverence. These must mate,
> And fuse with Jacob's mystic heart,
> To wrestle with the angel—Art.

("Art")

What is said here sounds very much like Coleridge's Romantic criticism, as it could be found, for example, in the *Biographia Literaria.* The reconciliation of opposites, the organic vitalist terms of life, pulsing, melting, fusing, and the heart, are all highly Coleridgean. Effort and struggle are more forcefully realized in Melville; one reason for this would be that in discussing artistic creation Coleridge generally had Shakespeare in mind as his ideal, whereas Melville is thinking of his own problems, in more specifically workmanlike terms. His Romanticism has come to be, however, the complex and carefully balanced Coleridgean doctrine and not the more daring and radical organicism typical of America, as it is represented in Emerson and Whitman. His "reverence for the Archetype" is possible to square with the organicist metaphor of growth, but it takes some doing; even, be it said, although the idea of the archetype can be found in the arch-organicist Blake. . . .

The body of poems unpublished in Melville's life-time lacks the coherence of his published volumes, for the most part, and these poems date from various, sometimes undetermined periods of his life from about 1859. The greater number of them presumably come from his old age. Two long poems, "In the Hostelry" and "Naples in the Time of Bomba," companion-pieces under the title of the *Marquis de Grandvin,* were probably written, however, between 1857 and 1859. They are drawn from Melville's visit to Naples, recorded in the *Journal of a Visit to Europe and the Levant.* A group of poems called *Weeds and Wildings with a Rose or Two* seems to be a mixture of relatively early and late with the late predominating.

With this uncertainty about dates it is impossible to trace any definite development of theme in Melville's unpublished poems, but for the most part they fall into thematic groups. A number celebrate the downtrodden weed, useless and in danger in a utilitarian world; the hedonist theme of the rose, on the other hand, is also prominent; among the more casual and relaxed pieces there are bird-poems and two Christmas poems. The problem of the Christian belief in immortal life arises significantly, as well as its counter-theme the golden age. Melville's preoccupation with ironic complexity appears in flower-and-skull images, usually in relatively early verse. Perhaps the largest group among these unpublished pieces attacks the utilitarian spirit of the age from various points of view, nostalgic, idealistic, hedonist, charitable.

From "The Themes of Melville's Later Poetry," *Tulane Studies in English,* 11 (1961), 65-86.

CHARLES WEIR, JR.

Malice Reconciled;
A Note on Melville's *Billy Budd*

A CURSORY epitome [of *Billy Budd*] indicates the possibility of complexity, and when the characteristics of Melville's mind and work are taken into consideration, the possibility becomes a certainty. The symbolic method which Melville had used with increasing predilection ever since the period of *Mardi* is obviously here at work, as is also Melville's preoccupation with the problem of sin, the difficulty of distinguishing good from evil, the arbitrary character of earthly justice—in brief, the moral nature of the Deity and his creatures. A closer inspection of *Billy Budd* reveals further that, in contrast to his earlier attempts, Melville has here succeeded in formulating a solution to the problem which is both morally and artistically satisfactory.

The purely physical action of the story is clear enough, and about its significant details there is never any doubt. To be sure, the ramifications of Claggart's plot to entrap Billy are hidden from the reader, but he realizes that there is a plot, which is all that is necessary. It is, therefore, with some consideration of the characters of the three principal actors that any analysis must begin.

II

Melville's delineation of Vere, though rapid, is for his purposes thorough. The two chief characteristics of the captain are intelligence and a sense of duty. Meditative, fond of philosophy and history, he is a man respected, if not understood or loved, by his fellow officers. Essentially he represents the active, speculative intellect, controlled by a deep-rooted instinct of responsibility to a law that transcends the individual. " 'With mankind,' he would say, 'forms, measured forms, are everything . . . .'" If a philosophical label for him is desired, that of a Christian Stoic will do very well. He is, it should be noted, the only major character in all Melville's work who is felt to be completely capable of coping with his environment.

Billy himself, in his capacity for accepting life, is related to Vere, with the important difference, however, that in him the intellectual quality of Vere is completely lacking. Billy, Melville tells us, is the "Handsome Sailor" of legend—the perfect physical man, the highest type of human animal. But he is also, the reader realizes, Rousseau's noble savage, and, one might add, Adam before the Fall. Completely without a knowledge of Evil, he is completely trusting. He is "one to whom not as yet had been proffered the questionable apple of knowledge." He accepts the world as it is, since it cannot occur to him to doubt that it is good or to imagine that it could be otherwise. He cannot believe that Claggart, who treats him so kindly, is actually his enemy: for him a man who smiles cannot be a villain. The concept of duplicity is beyond him; the possibility of ambiguity in any sphere he cannot even mentally formulate. It is not alone his defect in speech that keeps him from defending himself against Claggart's accusations; intellectually he is quite incapable of conducting such a defence, or even of realizing that such a defence could be conducted. His only possible reaction to all danger, including calumny, is action on his own plane—the physical. Against a lie, he has as weapon only a blow. His isolation from the average man is emphasized by his sudden appearance on board the *Indomitable*, as though dropped from heaven, and heightened by the fact that he is totally ignorant of his birthplace or parents. When, how, or why he came into being, he does not know, and he questions his genesis no more than he does his fate. He is the perfect symbol of trusting innocence "dropped into a world not without some man-traps and against whose subtleties simple courage lacking experience and address and without any touch of defensive ugliness, is of little avail; and where such innocence as man is capable of does yet, in a moral emergency, not always sharpen the faculties or enlighten the will."

Billy and Vere are characters easily grasped. Not so Claggart. "This portrait I essay, but shall never hit it," Melville wrote, and so far as many readers are concerned, with justice. Claggart's antecedents, like Billy's, are covered with mystery, but of a darker sort. There is about him an atmosphere both of distinguished birth and of a criminal past. He is handsome in a saturnine way, self-controlled—but not without effort, as Vere is—and intelligent: of all those on board, only he and Vere are capable of recognizing Billy's nature as the rare phenomenon it is. All critics have seen that in some manner he represents Evil, but not all have agreed as to what that manner is. The problem has been unduly confused by the obvious marks of homosexuality with which Melville has endowed him. Actually, that characteristic is not fundamental and will of itself not explain, as has been suggested, his aversion to Billy. We are not to suppose him plotting revenge for a disappointment in love; though Billy would surely have rejected his advances, actually there were none. He is a man endowed with "a depravity according to nature," Melville wrote: and in that capacity his hatred of Billy is, under any conditions, natural and absolute.[1]

No one has ever doubted that in writing *Billy Budd* Melville had a deeper intent than that of simply telling a story. Esoteric interpretations of the tale have been plentiful. The purity of Billy has seized the imagination of some readers, and this combined with the idea of him as a victim—a lamb led to the slaughter—has suggested to them an analogy with Christ. Hints at such

1. I do not mean to say that Claggart's homosexuality should, on a naturalistic level, be overlooked. To whatever degree it may serve to give the story reality it is important. I do, however, suggest that it has only the importance of any other detail designed to add to the realism of the narrative and that on the philosophical level it is not of importance.

an interpretation can be gathered from the text: fragments of the yardarm at which Billy is hanged are treasured by the sailors like bits of the True Cross, a mystic Father-Son relationship can be imagined between Billy and Vere, and a phrase from the description of Billy's execution can be twisted into a reference to the Ascension. That Melville intended such touches deliberately is, of course, possible; but a little reflection makes it evident that such a parallel in no way serves to illuminate the story. The innocence of Billy is by no means the innocence of Christ, and he neither voluntarily seeks his death nor directly serves any purpose by it. Actually, in none of Melville's novels—nor, it would seem, in his thought—does the idea of a redeemer play any part. Charles Olson has remarked that Christ is absent from *Moby-Dick;* he is equally absent from *Billy Budd.* The Supreme Power of Melville, if not always the Deity of the Old Testament, resembles him in his inaccessibility to man. Before his judgments man stands, accepting or revolting, but essentially helpless, without a mediator. Indeed, a closer parallel to the tragedy of Billy can be found, as Melville himself points out, in the story of Abraham and Isaac.

Billy Budd will most easily give up its secrets when considered in relation to Melville's earlier work. Beginning with *Mardi,* all Melville's major novels—*Moby-Dick, Pierre,* and *The Confidence Man*—concern themselves primarily with what [Yvor] Winters has called the problem of "moral navigation." The century-old antitheses of heavenly justice and earthly fallibility, sin and innocence, Heaven and Hell, God and the Devil dominate Melville's mind. Christian perfection or worldly-wise prudence, free-will or predestination, in which should a man place his belief? How can the concept of a just, all-perfect, all-powerful God be reconciled with the harsh reality of sin and suffering in his creation? How can the doctrine of the Church be reconciled with the reality of the world? These questionings, confused and unmethodical, pervade Melville's work. . . .

In *Billy Budd,* the eternal question [about existence] is again asked—and now for the first time answered. All the earlier elements are here. Like Pierre, Billy is the innocent man, like Pierre he learns the doubleness of the world, the evil reality that lurks beneath the smiling surface, like Pierre he attempts to answer its threat by action: he strikes out against the evil and meets defeat. Trusting innocence, naive faith unmoulded by experience, shipwrecks on reality.

Opposed to Billy is Claggart. In what does his evil consist? Partly at least in negation—denial, hate, contempt, "pale ire, envy and despair." Claggart is in some measure Ahab, a man possessing "the high perception" and hence denied "the low enjoying power." Like Ahab, he is "damned, most subtly and most malignantly! damned in the midst of Paradise." But Claggart is an Ahab who spiritually has never put to sea, who accepts the malignant spirit, lacking the firmness of purpose to track it to its utmost hiding place. It is his conviction of the hidden rot underlying the creation that inspires his hatred of Billy. It is mysterious, Melville admits: "For what can more partake of the mysterious than an antipathy spontaneous and profound such as is evoked in certain exceptional mortals by the mere aspect of some other mortal, however harmless he may be?—if not called forth by that very harmlessness itself." But for all its strangeness, it is none the less real. Claggart envies and execrates the pure spirit of Billy, that spirit which he instinctively knows "had in its simplicity never willed malice or experienced the reactionary bite of [the] serpent." And so that innocence must be degraded and broken: "With no power to annul the elemental evil in himself, though readily enough he could hide it; apprehending the good, but powerless to be it; a nature like Claggart's, surcharged with energy as such natures almost invariably are, what recourse is left to it but to recoil upon itself and like the scorpion for which the Creator alone is responsible, act out to the end the part allotted it." That Billy should pass, trusting and unscathed, through an evil world is a torment that Claggart cannot bear, a direct offence to him and his whole conception of man's life. In this bitterness, Claggart is Melville too, the Melville who wrote *The Confidence Man* and *Pierre,* the Melville who took a bitter delight in torturing his creation Pierre, in entwining him with a web of plots and ironic coincidences and leaving him physically and morally broken on a prison floor.

In *Billy Budd,* the tragedy of Pierre is repeated; but there is a final act, and another figure—that of Vere, Melville's final synthesis. He is distinct from Billy and above him by virtue of a superior mind; in particular, by virtue of a superior understanding of the world. Billy is without experience; Vere is amply provided with it, from books and from life. Claggart too resembles Vere in this, but with the all-important distinction that for him experience has been a bitter draught. Experience is the touchstone here. . . . Earlier in Melville there have been similar hints, hints which never reach profundity because of Melville's almost pathological desire to cling to the ideal of unstained innocence. But now Melville has reached a decision. Goodness and innocence are not of necessity inseparable: "Of such are the Kingdom of Heaven," Christ said, speaking of the little children, but their merit does not consist primarily in their ignorance of evil. The Ahabs are wrong in the conclusions which they draw from their experience of this world; the existence of evil need not call into question the existence of good. The Claggarts are even more wrong in their unhappy acceptance of that evil. In Melville's work, Vere stands alone as the complete moral man: aware of the spiritual dangers that beset humanity, pained by the occasional victories of the malign spirit, yet sustained by the conviction that man's salvation lies in following what measure of light is given to him, in upholding the law as he has received it. "Our vowed responsibility is in this: That however pitilessly that law may operate, we nevertheless adhere to it and administer it."

III

Essentially, of course, Vere's acceptance, like Billy's, must be a matter of faith. In *Mardi,* Taji, the questing spirit of man, had rejected the security of a simple faith and had pushed on into the void. But now Melville's period of reasoning, of wandering to and fro over the deserts of the mind, has passed.

It is not by a process of intellection that he brings the reader to his final conclusion, for no more than Vere can the reader attain it through demonstration. It is thus that in the pages of *Billy Budd* Melville's symbolic art reaches its highest peak. The genius for shaping the material world into an effective counterpart of the spiritual he had already amply shown [in *Moby-Dick*]. . . . It is by the same method that in *Billy Budd* Melville makes his climactic assertion of eternal justice.

The symbolism is drawn from two sources: external nature and the subtly glorified discipline of a man of war. With remarkable care and precision the touches are added one by one, the last coming in a sentence which in its fusion of form and content represents Melville's peak of achievement.

The process begins quietly, with a view of Billy lying in irons on the *Indomitable's* gun deck, awaiting execution. The deck is in semi-darkness; the guns, carriages, hempen breechings are a funereal black, but in the midst of them glimmers the whiteness of Billy's garments—like a shroud. The pale moonshine struggling to reach him is polluted by the "dirty yellow light" of the swinging lanterns. But slowly dawn comes, and with it the ship rouses into action. "A meek shy light appeared in the East, where stretched a diaphanous fleece of white furrowed vapour. That light slowly waxed. Suddenly *one bell* was struck aft, responded to by one louder metallic stroke from forward. It was four o'clock in the morning. Instantly the silver whistles were heard summoning all hands to witness punishment." The execution proceeds, marked by a fated dignity. "God bless Captain Vere," Billy exclaims "at the penultimate moment"; and the benediction is strangely echoed by the entranced witnesses.

> At the pronounced words and the spontaneous echo that voluminously rebounded them, Captain Vere, either through stoic self-control or a sort of momentary paralysis induced by emotional shock, stood erectly rigid as a musket in the ship-armour's rack.
>
> The hull, deliberately recovering from the periodic roll to leeward, was just regaining an even keel—when the last signal, the preconcerted dumb one, was given. At the same moment it chanced that the vapoury fleece hanging low in the East, was shot through with a soft glory as of the fleece of the Lamb of God seen in mystical vision; and simultaneously therewith, watched by the wedged mass of upturned faces, Billy ascended; and ascending, took the full rose of the dawn.
>
> In the pinioned figure, arrived at the yard-end, to the wonder of all no motion was apparent save that created by the slow roll of the hull, in moderate weather so majestic in a great ship heavy-cannoned.

Melville's first *tour de force* has been accomplished. The terrible danger of falling into bathos implicit in such a scene has been overcome by his grasp of reality. By itself, "the full rose of the dawn" would be impossible, but when it is tempered by the quiet, precise detail—"the slow roll of the hull, in moderate weather so majestic in a great ship heavy-cannoned"—the effect is

overwhelming. And Melville continues. "The silence at the moment of execution, and for a moment or two continuing thereafter (but emphasized by the
regular wash of the sea against the hull, or the flutter of a sail caused by the
helmsman's eyes being tempted astray), this emphasized silence was gradually
disturbed by a sound. . . . " The sound is the angry murmuring of the crew,
momentarily released from the dignity of the moment, questioning the justice
of the proceedings. And now Order asserts itself: "Shrill as the shriek of the
seahawk the whistles of the Boatswain and his Mates pierced that ominous low
sound, dissipating it"; and doubt yields to "the mechanism of discipline." The
body is prepared for burial, and, with the crew drawn up a second time, burial
takes place. Again nature serves symbolically, and again the symbolism is made
to seem natural by precise detail.

> But when the tilted plank let slide its freight into the sea, a second
> strange human murmur was heard—blended now with another so inarti-
> culate sound proceeding from certain larger sea-fowl, whose attention
> having been attracted by the peculiar commotion in the water resulting
> from the heavy sloped dive of the shotted hammock into the sea, flew
> screaming to the spot. So near the hull did they come, that the stridor
> or bony creak of their gaunt double-jointed pinions was audible. As the
> ship under light airs passed on, leaving the burial spot astern, they still
> kept circling it low down with the moving shadow of their outstretched
> wings and the cracked requiem of their cries.

The crew murmurs, and again, with drum-beat to quarters, discipline—"forms,
measured forms"—is exalted. The daily inspection takes place, the chaplain
performs the customary morning service, and as the drums beat retreat, "toned
by music and religious rites subserving the discipline and purpose of war, the
men in their wonted, orderly manner dispersed to the places allotted them
when not at the guns." Now is the climactic moment: even as Billy has been
glorified by the rosy dawn, so Vere and the ship, in which the law has been
accomplished and the rites observed, are glorified and approved by the risen
sun: "And now it was full day. The fleece of low-hanging vapour had vanished,
licked up by the sun that late had so glorified it. And the circumambient air
in the clearness of its serenity was like smooth white marble in the polished
block not yet removed from the marble-dealer's yard."

The paradox has been established: injustice may find its place within the
pattern of a larger, all-embracing divine righteousness.

From "Malice Reconciled; A Note on Melville's *Billy Budd*," *The University of Toronto Quarterly*, 13 (April 1944), 276-85.

SELECTED BIBLIOGRAPHY

Works

Editions

Billy Budd, Sailor (An Inside Narrative): Reading Text and Generic Text, Edited from the Manuscript with Introduction and Notes. Ed. Harrison Hayford and Merton M. Sealts, Jr. Chicago: Univ. of Chicago Press, 1962.

Complete Works. 7 of 14 vols. published to date. New York: Hendricks House, 1956-date.

Journal of a Visit to Europe and the Levant, October 11, 1856-May 6, 1857. Ed. Howard C. Horsford. Princeton: Princeton Univ. Press, 1955.

Journal of a Visit to London and the Continent, 1849-1850. Ed. Eleanor Melville Metcalf. Cambridge: Harvard Univ. Press, 1948.

The Works of Herman Melville. The Standard Edition. 16 vols. London: Constable, 1922-1924. Now a collector's item, but the volumes have been reproduced—New York: Russell & Russell, 1963.

The Writings of Herman Melville. The Northwestern-Newberry Edition, annotated. Ed. Harrison Hayford, Hershel Parker, and G. Thomas Tanselle. 5 of 15 vols. published to date. Chicago: Northwestern Univ. Press, 1967-date.

Selections

In addition to the many reprints of Melville's novels, useful selections are edited by Hennig Cohen (*Selected Poems*. Carbondale: Southern Illinois Univ. Press, 1964); Jay Leyda (*The Portable Melville*. New York: Viking, 1952).

Letters

Herman Melville: Cycle and Epicycle. Ed. Eleanor Melville Metcalf. Cambridge: Harvard Univ. Press, 1953.

The Letters of Herman Melville. Ed. Merrell R. Davis and William H. Gilman. New Haven, Conn.: Yale Univ. Press, 1960.

Biography and Criticism

Adams, R. P. "Romanticism and the American Renaissance." *American Literature*, 23 (Jan. 1952), 419-32.

Barrett, Laurence. "The Differences in Melville's Poetry." *Publications of the Modern Language Association*, 70 (Sept. 1955), 606-23.

Blackmur, R. P. "The Craft of Herman Melville: A Putative Statement." *The Expense of Greatness*. New York: Arrow Editions, 1940.

Boies, Jack Jay. *"The Whale* Without Epilogue." *Modern Language Quarterly*, 24 (June 1963), 172-76.

Braswell, William. *Melville's Religious Thought: An Essay in Interpretation*. Durham, N. C.: Duke Univ. Press, 1943.

Canaday, Nicholas, Jr. *Melville and Authority*. Gainesville: Univ. of Florida Press, 1968.

Chase, Richard. *Herman Melville: A Critical Study.* New York: Macmillan, 1949.

Fogle, Richard Harter. *Melville's Shorter Tales.* Norman: Univ. of Oklahoma Press, 1960.

Hillway, Tyrus. *Herman Melville.* New York: Twayne, 1963.

Hillway, Tyrus, and Luther S. Mansfield, eds. *Moby-Dick Centennial Essays.* Dallas, Texas: Southern Methodist Univ. Press, 1953.

Howard, Leon. *Herman Melville: A Biography.* Berkeley: Univ. of California Press, 1951.

Leyda, Jay. *The Melville Log: A Documentary Life of Herman Melville, 1819-1891.* 2 vols. New York: Harcourt, Brace, 1951.

Mason, Ronald. *The Spirit Above the Dust: A Study of Herman Melville.* London: John Lehmann, 1951.

Moorman, Charles. "Melville's *Pierre* and the Fortunate Fall." *American Literature,* 25 (Jan. 1953), 13-30.

Noone, John B., Jr. *"Billy Budd:* Two Concepts of Nature." *American Literature,* 29 (Jan. 1957), 249-62.

Osbourn, R. V. "The White Whale and the Absolute." *Essays in Criticism,* 6 (April 1956), 160-70.

Rosenberry, Edward Hoffman. *Melville and the Comic Spirit.* Cambridge: Harvard Univ. Press, 1955.

Sedgwick, William Ellery. *Herman Melville: The Tragedy of Mind.* Cambridge: Harvard Univ. Press, 1944.

Slater, Judith. "The Domestic Adventurer in Melville's Tales." *American Literature,* 37 (Nov. 1965), 267-79.

Warren, Robert Penn. "Melville's Poems." *Southern Review,* N. S., 3 (Oct. 1967), 799-855.

Weaver, Raymond. *Herman Melville: Mariner and Mystic.* 1921; rpt. New York: Pageant, 1960.

Winters, Yvor. "Herman Melville and the Problems of Moral Navigation," *Maule's Curse: Seven Studies in the History of American Obscurantism.* 1938; rpt. *In Defense of Reason,* New York: The Swallow Press and William Morrow, 1947.

Wright, Nathalia. *Melville's Use of the Bible.* Durham, N. C.: Duke Univ. Press, 1949.